Major Khleber Miller Van Zandt

A
BANKING
HISTORY OF TEXAS
1835 - 1929

BY
AVERY LUVERE CARLSON, PH.D.
Department of Business Administration,
Texas Christian University

Edited by Michelle M. Haas

Copano Bay Press
2007

Second Edition, Revised 2007

ISBN 978-0-9767799-1-9

Library of Congress Control Number: 2007923439

TO THE MEMORY OF
ETHEL HUTCHISON HAMACHER
NOVEMBER 28, 1882 – MARCH 4, 1929,
WHO PERSUADED ME TO GO
TO COLLEGE

TABLE OF CONTENTS

EDITOR'S NOTE

Dr. Carlson's writing is filled with valuable information not readily available elsewhere and is certainly worthy of reaching new generations of readers interested in the tumultuous and often melodramatic history of banking in Texas. Those who study Texas history learn of the phenomenal resources of our vast land and of the swashbuckling endeavors of our pioneering forebears, but we often don't hear much about the institutions that helped facilitate the economic growth of this state. Dr. Carlson's aim was to recognize those individuals and firms that embraced the monumental task of providing dependable banks to a widely distributed and fiercely independent people.

The majority of Dr. Carlson's original text is preserved in this revised edition, but the arrangement has been altered somewhat to present the book in a fashion that renders the facts more accessible. A new index has also been added to further this cause. As a general rule, the language has not been updated to allow the text to retain its 1920s vernacular. The only major enhancements made were those that would do justice to Dr. Carlson's hard work by making his presentation of the facts more readable.

Michelle M. Haas
Seven Palms - Rockport, Texas

INTRODUCTION
By Peter Molyneaux

This volume is just what its title indicates: a history of the banking systems of Texas. It is the result of exhaustive research by Dr. Carlson, and its value lies chiefly in that it represents a narrative presentation of all the essential facts, so far as the protracted searching of a trained investigator could bring them to light. So well has Dr. Carlson performed his task, that no one in the future who undertakes to tell the story of Texas banking can escape the necessity of using this little work as a guide, for it is doubtful that any important or considerable data will be brought to light which Dr. Carlson has not thoroughly considered and given its due weight and proper place in the story.

It is needless to say that Dr. Carlson's chief objective has been to present the facts, and not primarily to write an interesting narrative. And yet there is much in these pages which even the casual reader will find of interest. However, it is in order to say that it is as an authentic record that the book is valuable. Dr. Carlson has not attempted to write "literature" nor to beguile his readers during idle hours. Rather has he attempted to follow the financial adventures of a people in a new land, from frontier days to the highly organized civilization which has developed during a period of nearly a century.

The Fort Worth National Bank has published this work in memory of its founder and presiding head during most of its existence, Major K. M. Van Zandt. The book was completed during Major Van Zandt's lifetime when he was still actively a part of the Texas banking system, and it has been deemed proper to leave it just as it came from the author's hand, without modifying such references to Major Van Zandt and his work as it originally contained. The author very justly calls Major Van Zandt "Texas's greatest living banker." Major Van Zandt was all of that at the time the work was completed and it has been thought fitting to let the statement stand just as it was written.

When Major Van Zandt reached the end of his earthly labors on the morning of March 19, 1930, the writer of this introductory word set forth his own estimate of the veteran banker's life and work in a short editorial in *Texas Weekly*. It was a spontaneous expression of honest conviction, and as such, it is appended below in the belief that no more deliberate estimate would be quite as appropriate in the present connection. It reads as follows:

A well-spent life came to a close when Major K. M. Van Zandt passed away at Fort Worth on Wednesday morning. If it is true, as Emerson has said, that an institution is the lengthened shadow of a man, then surely the Fort Worth National Bank is the embodiment of Major Van Zandt's more than fifty years of service as its head, and will stand as his monument as long as the financial system of Texas stands. For in building that splendid institution, he built into the very structure of the State's financial system, and Texas banking owes to him what it owes to few other men in its history. Major Van Zandt's long service as a citizen of Fort Worth, a service which led the people of that city to bestow upon him, with appropriate justice, the title of 'first citizen', constitutes an unusual record of disinterested public devotion. His record as a soldier of the Confederacy during the Civil War sheds luster upon the name of a worthy son of a truly distinguished father. These alone would have set him apart among men. But too frequently the service of such men in laying the economic foundations of civilization is minimized, and such a notable example of this kind of service is supplied by the career of Major Van Zandt as a banker that it should be emphasized accordingly.

Major Van Zandt was one of the founders of the Texas banking system, and throughout the history of that system he has been the embodiment of all those elements that go into the making of a trustworthy custodian of a community's credit, and an inspiring leader in the establishment of sound financial practice. The place of such a man in the history of civilization in the region in which he lived and labored could hardly be set too high. Such men seldom receive the plaudits of the multitude, though few others may be justly said more richly to deserve them. There will be many to praise Major Van Zandt for his virtues as a citizen, and for his valor as a soldier, and he merited abundantly all such praise they may bestow. But it will be his influence as a master banker of sterling worth and inspiring qualities of leadership which will be most intimately interwoven in the future destiny of Texas. And that influence will be present in the financial structure of the State after the very names of the youngest children who knew him have been forgotten by their own descendants. Of such enduring quality are the fruits of a well-spent life devoted to such service.

THE REPUBLIC ERA AND
EARLY STATEHOOD

The Constitution of the Republic of Texas was silent on the subject of banks, although it did contain a provision granting Congress the power "to coin money, regulate the value thereof and of foreign coins, but nothing but gold and silver shall be made a lawful tender." It is clear that the Congress had in mind the establishment of a banking system, for in a joint resolution for the relief of Thomas F. McKinney and Samuel M. Williams passed in 1836, the Secretary of the Treasury was authorized "to negotiate a loan from any bank or banks that may be established in this republic of sufficient amount for the payment of all just claims held by Messrs. McKinney and Williams against this government." McKinney and Williams had drawn on their credit in the United States in order to raise money to fund the revolution in Texas. These gentlemen played a vital role in the business and banking history of Texas, and it is all too fitting that they were the subjects of such legislation in the Republic's infancy.

At the time of the joint resolution, a bank had already been chartered in Texas by S. M. Williams himself. Williams had obtained a charter from the Congress of the Mexican State of Coahuila y Texas at Monclova for the *Banco de Commercia y Agricultura* in April 1835. It is believed that this charter was granted by the Mexican authorities partly as a concession to the rebellious Texans in an attempt to stave off revolution. While the Commercial and Agricultural Bank did not open until after statehood, the Mexican charter was recognized by the Republic of Texas. Williams, a Rhode Island native born in 1795, had served as secretary to General Andrew Jackson. In 1821 he immigrated to San Felipe de Austin, where in 1824 he secured the position of clerk, and later secretary, to Stephen F. Austin. During his tenure with Austin, Williams had frequent business dealings with Thomas F. McKinney. Just before the revolution started, Williams and McKinney formed a partnership in the mercantile business at Quintana, Texas at the mouth of the Brazos river. In 1838 this firm opened a business at Galveston, where they built the first wharf, constructed the first warehouse, and owned the first boat, the *Lafitte*.

The mercantile firm of McKinney & Williams prospered. They transacted a general commission business and gradually assumed banking functions. Their business dealings extended to New Orleans and Philadelphia. The firm had some difficulties in meeting their obligations promptly, a fact which is shown by the protested drafts in the Samuel M. Williams manuscript collection in the Rosenberg Library at Galveston, which this writer examined in detail. At this time, gold and silver were scarce in Texas, and there were no banks in operation. In order to carry on their mercantile business, McKinney and Williams found it necessary to extend credit to their customers, accept drafts and discount promissory notes. Numerous drafts and notes are found in the Williams papers at Galveston.

The firm was active in raising funds for provisional government of the struggling Republic of Texas. In 1835, they were called upon to raise $100,000 for the Republic. Arrangements were made for the government to draw on them in favor of its foreign agents and McKinney served as fiscal agent of the government. The firm imported merchandise extensively and continued to carry on a mercantile and commission business together with certain banking functions, while also serving as the main financial support for the Republic of Texas. Meanwhile, numerous unsuccessful attempts were made to raise the minimum capital to open the Commercial and Agricultural Bank prior to statehood.

Other banking projects were brought forward during the days of the Republic. A proposal to incorporate a hotel and bathhouse with banking privileges at Velasco was made. It was also proposed to incorporate an Internal Improvement and Banking Company at Houston. The organization of a railroad and banking company was also suggested but none of these proposals ever materialized. In 1838, the Texas Railroad Navigation and Banking Company was chartered with a $5,000,000 capital. This institution was to be a bank of issue and it was required to redeem its notes on demand in gold or silver. The incorporators, however, were unable to raise the necessary $25,000 in specie to be paid into the Texas treasury before the institution could open. Consequently, this institution never functioned. Numerous other banking, insurance and railroad companies were chartered, only to suffer a stillbirth for lack of capital.

President Mirabeau B. Lamar had ambitious plans for the organization of a national bank of Texas. In a message to the Congress of the Republic on December 31, 1838 he urged the organization of such an institution by the government. This was to be a bank of deposit and issue, and its bills were to be secured by land, specie and the public credit. At this time, many monetary and banking controversies were raging in the United States, and many worthless banknotes were finding their way to Texas. In addition, the Republic of Texas had virtually converted itself into a bank of issue by emitting thousands of dollars in paper money. The unsound condition of the currency had produced many economic and social maladjustments in Texas, and the people were interested in any scheme that promised relief. Lamar believed that the proposed National Bank of Texas would combine the three essential elements for a safe bank: land, specie, and the public faith. He proposed a bank with branches throughout the Republic, and correspondents in the United States and Europe. In his address to the Congress, he envisioned a bank in operation "dispersing a sound circulating medium which would always be convertible into specie without discount."

Unfortunately, at this time, the Republic of Texas had no specie and its credit was near the vanishing point while its boundless acres of fertile land had no market value. The Congress was able to see the impossibility of establishing a successful national bank under the prevailing economic conditions and in 1839 rejected the bill by a vote of sixteen to fourteen. Meanwhile the firm of McKinney and Williams at Galveston continued to serve as banker for the people and the government.

In 1841 Congress authorized this firm to issue $30,000 in notes to circulate as money. The security for these notes was mortgages on real estate and on Negroes, the amount of the mortgages to be limited to 50 percent of the value of the property. This power given to a private concern to issue paper money represents one of the few cases of such in banking history. It was granted to this firm in view of their sound record as private bankers and their large advances to the government in its earlier days. However, there was much opposition in Texas at this time to the plan of allowing banks to issue paper money since many banks in the U.S. had abused the privilege and flooded the country with worthless paper. Accordingly, in 1844 the Congress of the Republic repealed all laws granting authority to any persons or corporation the right to emit bills or promissory notes to circulate as money. In doing so, the Republic proceeded to suppress all banks and to convert itself into a bank of issue by flooding the country with paper money. The Republic launched a policy of monetary inflation in 1837 which led to financial ruin, and eventually annexation to the United States and the final adjustment of her prorated $7,775,000 debt on the basis of 76.9 cents on the dollar.

During the period of the Republic, many foreign bank notes and numerous private promissory notes circulated in Texas. In fact, there is evidence that the promissory note was used as a basis for credit in Austin during the Mexican regime. Between 1835 and 1837 many banknotes were brought to Texas by immigrants from Mississippi and other states. There were numerous wildcat state banks in Mississippi, Louisiana, Tennessee, Alabama and Georgia. Their paper found its way to Texas and usually circulated at a depreciated rate. The Panic of 1837 marked the downfall of many of these unsound banks. Their already depreciated currency was now worthless and Texans, already suspicious of paper currency now had complete distrust for it.

During this time, extensive use was made of the promissory note by the people of Texas. In the absence of banking facilities, this instrument proved a convenient method of deferring the payment of many business obligations. These notes were customarily transferred by endorsement. They were frequently payable at sight or one day after date, although 60-day, 90-day, and 120-day paper was common. They varied in amount from a few dollars up to $5,000. The use of negotiable instruments of this type became so common that Congress was compelled to enact legislation in 1836 and in 1840 governing their circulation. McKinney and Williams at Galveston discounted many of these notes and thus extended credit to numerous people.

The Constitutional Convention of 1845 clearly reflected public opinion when it wrote into the Constitution language prohibiting the establishment of banks and the issue of paper money entirely. The first State Constitution contained the following: "No corporate body shall hereafter be created, renewed, or extended with banking or discounting privileges. ... The Legislature shall prohibit by law individuals from issuing bills, checks, or promissory notes, or other paper, to circulate as money".

These provisions were adopted only after vehement debate. Most of the delegates to the conventions were opposed to banks but there was, nonetheless, disagreement over the question of incorporating a constitutional prohibition. In the end, the opposition to banks won the day and the language prohibiting them made it into the document. Instead of solving the economic and monetary troubles of the people, this policy retarded the growth of the economic interests of the state for many years. The anti-bank attitude of Texans and their opposition to paper money at this time mirrored public opinion on the same question in many western states. But the growing agricultural and industrial interests of the state had to be financed in some way. Dependable banks were necessary.

Texas was primarily a rural state in the antebellum era. There were but twenty-three towns enumerated on the census of 1850, only five of which had a population of over 1,000 people. These towns were Galveston with 4,177 people, San Antonio with 3,488 persons, Houston with 2,396 people, New Braunfels with a population of 1,298 and Marshall, a village of

1,189 people. Only 9.5 percent of the state's 212,592 citizens lived in the towns. The remaining 90.5 percent of the people were scattered over the 262,398 square miles of territory in the state. The financial needs of these people were vastly different from the necessities of the five and one-half million people who dwell in the same region today.

During the first fifteen years of statehood, there were numerous monetary and economic problems which complicated the social lives of Texans. Public opinion in the state remained strongly against banks and paper money. This strange attitude was due, in part, to the negative experiences of the people with the worthless and depreciated banknotes issued by southern banks. It was also due, however, to the disastrous monetary results of the unchecked issue of treasury notes, audited drafts, and various other types of paper money issued by the Republic of Texas. Nor was the passing of counterfeit bills uncommon in early Texas. In 1857, for instance, a stranger purchased a pair of boots from a mercantile firm in Waco and presented a $50 banknote on the Union Bank of Louisiana as payment. The clerk took the bill out on the street to get it changed. A one-eyed man, who was also hard of hearing, but who declared he was a good judge of paper money, gave the clerk gold for the instrument which later proved to be counterfeit. As a result, gold and silver were the only money in which the people had complete confidence.

Gold and silver had long been recognized as basic money in this region. According to William A. Gouge of Philadelphia, who visited Texas in 1852 and wrote a gem of a volume called *The Fiscal History of Texas*, "the currency of Mexican Texas consisted of gold and silver. Money was scarce in Texas only when compared with Mexico, while it was plentiful when compared with most newly settled countries." According to Gouge, a large portion of the money in circulation consisted of "hammered dollars," which were valued at about ninety cents in United States money. These coins were old Spanish silver dollars from which the royal effigy had been defaced by the Mexicans as an expression of hatred toward the old Spanish rulers whose profile the coins bore, and to prevent their exportation. These Spanish metallic coins were first introduced in Mexico in 1520 and many of them were struck at a mint established in Mexico City in 1535. The coins struck at this mint in 1537 were known as *moneda macuquina*. Two centuries later a new mint was established in Mexico City and between 1734 and 1771, many coins bearing the Spanish coat of arms supported between two pillars of Hercules were struck at this mint. These coins were known as *moneda columnaria*. Prior to 1821, coins bearing the effigy of the King were circulated. They were known as *moneda de busto*. Later, the profile of Emperor Augustin de Iturbide was placed on the Mexican coins. The *Morelos peso* issued between 1811 and 1814 was a copper coin. In addition, the *rial*, a gold coin valued at ten shillings, and the Spanish *real* valued at 10 to 12 1/2 cents were used in Mexican Texas. The *real de vellón*, a $1.20 peso piece, also appeared in Texas. The currency in circulation in Texas under the Mexican regime was chiefly silver. Mexico issued no paper money. The only paper money in circulation at this time was bills of wildcat American banks, which found their way to Texas and which helped Texans to form unfavorable opinions of paper money.

There was only one chartered bank in operation in Texas prior to the Civil War and there was not one private banker in the state devoting his full time to banking. There were, however, a number of commission firms in Galveston and Austin in 1859, who handled bills and bank checks on southern banks, and who dealt in domestic and foreign exchange. A firm of lawyers in Palestine advertised in the *Texas Almanac* that "in the absence of banks and paper currency, we connected with our office two years ago the feature of buying and selling exchange. All payments by us are represented by sight drafts on Galveston, New Orleans and New York." A number of cotton merchants in Galveston advertised that they were prepared to make advancements on cotton and deal in domestic and foreign exchange. A land and collecting agent at Galveston advertised that "bills of the Bank of Louisiana would be received at par."

Reports in the 1859 *Texas Almanac* from various counties throughout Texas indicated that gold and silver were the prevailing types of currency and that the general population still opposed banks. In the absence of banks, the promissory note, although outlawed, continued to play an important part in the business transactions of antebellum Texas. Numerous cases involving this instrument are found in the reports of the Supreme Court of Texas for this period.

While most early Texans were predominantly anti-bank, there were many prominent citizens who believed in banks and who viewed banks as a solution to the state's monetary woes rather than an additional problem. In an able address delivered at Round Top, on February 6, 1858, Colonel C. H. Taylor of Cherokee Place argued for a state banking system in Texas. His address was published in the *Galveston Weekly News* on June 29, 1858 and represents a learned discourse on the question. Many newspapers of the day also weighed in on the issue. *The Houston Telegraph* and Galveston papers were notably in favor of a state banking system while the *Austin State Gazette* voiced opposition to the proposition. While the young state would have to wait until the late 1860s to see the charter of state banks, private banks would flourish in Texas in their stead.

THE COMMERCIAL AND AGRICULTURAL BANK: PIONEERING INSTITUTION

On April 30, 1835, just before the revolution which separated Texas from Mexico had its beginnings, Samuel May Williams applied to the Congress of the combined State of Coahuila and Texas at Monclova for a bank charter. The Mexican authorities granted Williams a charter for the *Banco de Commercia y Agricultura*. This charter was officially recognized by the Republic of Texas when legislation was enacted on December 10, 1836, providing for the selection of a commission to aid in establishing the bank. A translation of this charter may be found in Gammel's *Laws of Texas*, Vol. I, p. 406. Another translation is set forth in the case of *State v. Samuel M. Williams*, found in *Texas Reports*, Vol. VIII, p. 266. A third is found in the Rosenberg Library at Galveston. Not all of these translations agree in their exact wording, but the substance of the charter was as follows:

> (1) The bank was chartered for twenty years with Williams as empresario or promoter.
> (2) The maximum capital was placed at $1,000,000 but the bank was authorized to open when $300,000 had been subscribed to the capital stock and at least $100,000 had been placed in the vaults. Subscriptions were to be secured by real estate.
> (3) There were to be eight directors, each of whom was a citizen of the state and the owner of at least five shares of stock. Each could hold office for one year.
> (4) Each share was entitled to one vote but no subscriber was entitled to more than fifty votes.
> (5) The bank was to be a bank of issue. It was authorized to issue banknotes, signed by the president and cashier, and secured by the capital of the institution.
> (6) The bank was authorized to loan money at a maximum rate of 8 percent on six-month loans, and 10 percent on loans for a longer period. Collateral security for loans was permitted.

(7) The bank was authorized to establish branches in any part of the state.

(8) The bank was to be called the Commercial and Agricultural Bank. It was to be established in the Department of the Brazos and was to be examined annually.

During the period of the Republic of Texas, McKinney & Williams continued their commission and mercantile business but the charter for the new bank was not used. Williams and McKinney planned frequently to open the new bank but they were unable to raise the necessary funds. The disturbed political conditions involved in placing the new Republic on its feet, together with economic maladjustments which prevailed in Texas and throughout the United States in the 1830s and early 1840s were not conducive to the promotion of a bank in Texas. Money was scarce, most of the people of the country were exceedingly poor and capital hesitated to migrate to the farthing frontier known as Texas.

In order to secure the necessary $100,000 in specie to open the bank, McKinney and Williams looked to their friends in the United States. This amount of money was considered an enormous sum in those days. In 1835 and 1836 the necessary $100,000 was promised but the subscribers, most of whom lived in the United States, became financially embarrassed by the tumultuous economic conditions resulting in the Panic of 1837 and were unable to deliver the specie.

Meanwhile extensive preparations had been made to open the institution. A book of blank checks with the name "Commercial and Agricultural Bank" together with the partial date 183_ printed thereon was secured. This book is now on exhibition in the Rosenberg Library at Galveston. Apparently, the blanks were not used until the late 1850s, because the year on the stubs had been changed to 1859. The firm of McKinney and Williams made desperate efforts to raise the necessary specie when funds failed to arrive from the northeast. McKinney even made a trip to New Orleans to secure gold and silver. When he arrived there, he found the New Orleans banks had

COMMERCIAL & AGRICULTURAL BANK

suspended specie payment. Specie could not be obtained. The firm was urged to issue their own paper in exchange for specie and make a technical compliance with the charter but they refused absolutely to open the bank on any other than a safe basis. Stock could not be sold in Texas or any other place. Consequently, these early efforts to open the bank met with disappointment.

After twelve years of negotiation and struggling, the bank was finally opened on December 30, 1847. Niles F. Smith was present at the opening ceremonies to represent the State of Texas and count the cash in the vault. He certified that the vault contained $100,000 in specie at that time. The institution opened with Samuel May Williams as president and J. M. McMillen as cashier. These men, together with J. A. Reynolds, Jesse J. Davis, Jacob L. Briggs, Michael B. Menard, George Ball, and Henry Hubbell, constituted the first board of directors. This bank was located on the corner of Market and 23rd Street in Galveston and was the first incorporated bank established in Texas.

It does not appear that the capital of this bank ever exceeded $300,000 and information is lacking as to what portion of the subscribed capital was actually paid up. No financial statements of the bank appear to be in existence at the present time. An extensive search made by this writer through the old manuscript letters in the Samuel May Williams collection in the Rosenberg Library at Galveston failed to unearth such facts. The bank never advertised in the daily newspapers, hence only meager information is available concerning its career. The bank was in need of more capital in 1849, according to a letter written by the former cashier, McMillen, to President Williams, complimenting him on "the good appearance of the bank's balance sheet," and suggesting that the institution would become more profitable, "when [it had] sufficient real capital."

The opening of the Commercial and Agricultural Bank at Galveston in 1847 attracted considerable interest in business circles throughout the state. President Williams received many letters congratulating him on the fine beginning of his bank. One enthusiastic writer compared the institution to "an engine of enormous power" and ventured to suggest that the bank confine its operations to strictly business paper and avoid all forms of speculation.

After the bank opened, letters poured in from various Texas towns from persons who wanted to borrow money. The Williams collection of manuscript letters in the Rosenberg Library contains many such letters. One letter of interest was written by a college president in Grimes County who had landed in Galveston upon returning from a visit to his family in the northeast. He was broke and begged for a loan of ten dollars "to carry me home to my family." He made numerous promises to repay the money as soon as he got home. The money was repaid five days later. As a college president, he believed in maintaining his personal credit to use in emergencies such as this. Many people in Texas today might profit by this fine example.

The Williams manuscript collection contains many letters from people in stranded circumstances asking for small loans. Multitudes of people landed in Galveston in the 1840s on their journey to the interior of Texas. Many of them were dead broke and were forced to prevail on the bank for funds. These requests were freely granted by Williams. An insight into the remarkable character of Samuel May Williams is revealed by one modest-looking letter in the Williams manuscript collection written in 1848. A young man had fallen ill in Galveston in that year and he was without funds. Although Williams did not know the boy or his family, he gave the young man his personal attention, nursed him back to health and shortly thereafter, received a grateful letter from the boy's father, Warren Jenkins of Cleveland, Ohio.

Many requests for loans ranging from $25 to $1,000 for business purposes were made by people from all sections of the state, doubtless in more than a few cases, by irresponsible individuals. Many of the borrowers had difficulty in meeting their obligations to the bank because of the unfavorable economic

conditions prevailing at the time. One customer wrote a pa-
thetic letter to Williams, during the California Gold Rush,
stating that he was in the bank that morning, January 28, 1849,
to explain that he could not pay up at this time but that he
hoped to redeem his credit standing by going west to dig for
gold. About the same time, another borrower wrote a letter
"pledging his word and honor" that he would pay his note at
the bank within a year. He could not pay now, he stated, as his
family was suffering for the necessities of life. It is difficult for
people of today to appreciate the sufferings of these early
Texans. The tone of all these letters reveals the high moral
consciousness and noble character of the people who wrote
them. This writer did not find a single letter in the entire
Williams collection that was written in undignified language
or that reflected anything but high purposes.

No information was unearthed concerning the total deposits
of the Commercial and Agricultural Bank. However, numerous drafts and receipts indicated that the institution received
deposits ranging from $5 to $1,000 from persons scattered
throughout the state. For instance, in 1848 two drafts for $400
and $600 respectively were received from Cameron and, about
the same time, a deposit of $800 was received from San Anto-
nio. This is a testament to the faith that many Texans had in the
pioneering institution.

A demand for branches also developed in various progres-
sive towns of Texas. In 1848, a group of eighteen citizens of
Huntsville petitioned Samuel May Williams for a branch of the
bank. They represented that their community was "a highly
agricultural region." Productive agricultural regions, such as
the Huntsville area, could have proven to be extremely profit-
able branch locations. In the same year, a letter was received
from Trinity River, near Smithfield, in which the writer offered
to serve as agent of the bank at that place. He declared that the
cotton growers in his section of the state were sacrificing their
product for lack of banking facilities.

Despite the demand for branches of the Commercial and
Agricultural Bank, only one branch of the institution was ever

opened. Shortly after the Galveston bank opened, a branch was established at Brownsville, a small town in the extreme southern part of the state. This bank was located on the site now occupied by the Texas Bank & Trust Company in that town. The old vault is still in use by the latter bank, according to Bob Neale of Brownsville.

The Brownsville branch was placed in the charge of James N. Reynolds, who was also a director of the bank. He was designated as president as a matter of courtesy, although he declined to serve as executive president. Williams was the active president of this institution. In 1850, when a deposit of $11,000 was made in this bank, Warren Jenkins was acting as cashier and Theodore F. Brewer was engaged as bookkeeper. In 1852, John P. Couthorne was acting as agent of the Brownsville branch. These facts are found in the Williams manuscript collection and in a decision of the Texas Supreme Court in *Commercial Agricultural Bank v. Jones*, involving the bank's right to collect the deposit.

The branch at Brownsville carried on a rather large volume of business. It was established at this southerly point to serve Mexican-American interests but the Mexicans refused the bank's paper. They seemed to prefer their own hammered dollars. The bank and its singular branch were managed conservatively by Williams. In a letter to Couthorne written in 1852, Williams directed the agent "not to pay drafts or orders, nor discount notes in the hazardous business of mining. . .You must therefore stop that matter and proceed no further." At this time, we also find him writing that "the suit now pending in the Supreme Court makes me cautious. I devote my time to collecting and statements without creating any new business that might prevent a prompt winding up of the affairs of the bank should the opinion of the Supreme Court be adverse. You will not permit any discounts to anyone, until I am able to inform you whether we are to wind up our affairs, or whether we are to proceed further in our business. You are personally responsible to me, and to no one else, for all the transactions that may take place involving the branch bank."

Although only one branch of the institution was established in Texas, plans were worked out for the opening of agencies in New Orleans, Akron and elsewhere. J. M. McMillen was shortly succeeded as cashier at Galveston by Henry Jenkins and, in 1848, appeared in New Orleans in the interest of the bank. The following year, he wrote Williams concerning twenty-five sheets of banknotes that he was sending from Akron, Ohio. This letter indicates that McMillen still had authority to sign the banknotes as cashier. Warrick Martin was appointed agent of the bank at New Orleans, while Joseph L. Lake became the New York agent.

The bank at Galveston had occasional difficulties in maintaining the confidence of the people. While there is no evidence that the bank ever failed to meet its obligations on demand, rumors persisted that the bank was experiencing difficulties. In 1848, a man at Bastrop wrote to Williams and asked the question, "Why don't the bank circulate something to refute the many falsehoods circulated about it?" Williams replied, "The bank will prove its worth in time." President Williams evidently believed that prompt redemption of obligations on demand was the best method of stimulating public confidence in a bank. The wisdom in this policy is not disputed today.

Various estimates have been made as to the volume of notes the Commercial and Agricultural Bank put into circulation. In one letter from McMillen to Williams, the former stated that he had signed twenty-five sheets of $100, $50 and $20 banknotes, and he made reference to $200,000 in certificates previously signed. The bank also placed in circulation a number of banknotes, signed by S. M. Williams and J. M. McMillen, cashier, bearing the promise of the bank to pay "one dollar to the bearer on demand." One of these banknotes, in the amount of one dollar issued on January 1, 1848, is on exhibition in the Rosenberg Library. It is printed on one side only and bears the profile of George Washington, the figures of two sailing vessels, three steamers with side wheels and the figure of a tree. It is three by seven inches in size. The Williams manuscript collection also contains numerous cashier's checks, indicating that liberal use was made of this instrument. The numerous endorsements on these checks indicates that they passed through many hands.

The Commercial and Agricultural Bank carried on extensive business with other financial institutions in Galveston and in Houston, as well as in New Orleans. Cancelled checks and drafts bearing dates in the 1850s indicate that this bank maintained business relations with R. & D. G. Mills of Galveston, R. S. Mills & Brother of Montgomery, Alabama, B. A. Shepherd Exchange and Collection Office in Houston, Ball, Hutchings & Co. of Galveston, etc.

The first bank to operate in Texas ultimately collapsed under the weight of litigation brought against the institution in the 1850s in conjunction with extensive anti-bank legislation. The manuscript collection indicates that members of the Williams family were rightfully distraught about the bank and the swirling litigation. "If the worst comes, if there is anything I have detested it has been the Bank's connection with its influence over our family interest and quietude," one son wrote on January 27, 1857.

Several suits had been filed against the bank challenging its issuance of money and even questioning the validity of its charter. The bank and Samuel May Williams prevailed in the courts until 1857, when Williams was fined thousands of dollars for passing fifty $1 banknotes. Robert Mills, whose Galveston firm was also being rigorously challenged in the courts, was being similarly penalized. When Mills lost his court case, Williams's lawyers became worried and advised him to plea bargain and accept a fine of $2,000 for passing one bank note, thus setting the stage for future appeals. Williams would not live to witness the unfavorable results of the appeal, however, for on September 13, 1858, he died. Shortly after his death, the Texas Supreme Court nullified the bank's original charter on the grounds that the bank didn't begin operations until 1848, three years after the State Constitution had prohibited such activities.

The Commercial and Agricultural Bank closed its doors and its assets were liquidated. Presumably, the Brownsville branch closed at the same time. The good will of the institution passed to Ball, Hutchings & Company, which continues as a private bank in Galveston to this day. The gigantic key to the vault of the bank is on exhibition in the Rosenberg Library. Thus ended the first experiment with a chartered bank in Texas. The examples of conservative banking set by this pioneer Texas banker of unimpeachable character may well be studied by the bankers of today. All Texas should honor the name of Samuel May Williams.

PRIVATE BANKS

Early business concerns in Texas combined the dry goods, bakery and hardware businesses with the commission and banking business. In many eastern states, early banks were closely associated with the railroads. A start was made along this line in Texas but banking naturally developed out of the mercantile and commission business instead. These mercantile and commission merchants were compelled to perform banking functions in order to extend their trade. In the absence of adequate commercial banks, they served as retailers, commission merchants, factors, insurance agents, and bankers.

In southern states, the practice of making advances on cotton had existed for many years. In antebellum Texas, the cotton factors, commission merchants and a few private bankers continued the practice of making advances to the planters, whose crops they purchased. Mortgages on growing crops on the basis of ten dollars per expected bale with interest at 10 to 15 percent was the prevailing rule.

Since Galveston was the leading seaport and outlet for Texas products, financial agents developed first at this point out of necessity. As the agricultural development extended to the interior, other financial agencies of a primitive character were created to serve the needs of the people inland. The banking business in Texas, in common with banking in other American states, was primitive in character before the Civil War. These pioneer bankers, however, were laying the foundation for a banking system that has become today an outstanding institution. Texas owes much to her pioneer bankers.

The financial needs of the people in the interior of Texas were initially met by money lenders located in its various villages. The growing industrial and agricultural life of the interior called for credit facilities. This situation fostered the growth of money lenders in the various counties. These money lenders were the forerunners of the private bankers who dominated the banking business in the state until the dawn of the twentieth century. In 1858, there were estimated to be 2,638 such money lenders in Texas. Their total loans subject to taxation were reported at nearly $3,000,000. Eighty-seven counties reported 2,157 money lenders with total loans of approximately $2,500,000. Their geographical distribution ranged from one in Atascosa County, who reported loans of $500, to 105 in Dallas County with loans of $61,207, according to the *Texas Almanac* for 1858. In 1859 there were 3,021 money lenders with loans in excess of $3,000,000. The average number of money lenders per county in the 109 counties reporting was twenty-eight. These money lenders were taxed at the rate of twenty cents per $100 on their loans, although other property in Texas was taxed at the rate of twelve and a half cents per $100 on its value.

In addition to the firm of McKinney and Williams, there were several other mercantile firms and commission houses that engaged in banking as a sideline in the 1850s. The house of R. & D. G. Mills of Galveston was one of the most noted institutions of this period. In addition to serving as cotton factors and general commission merchants, they also dealt in money and foreign and domestic exchange. This firm was a partnership consisting of Robert Mills, David G. Mills, and John W. Jokusch. Robert Mills was also a partner in the firm of Mills, McDowell & Company of New York City, as well as McDowell, Mills & Company of New Orleans. These three firms were so closely associated that much of their paper passed through all three concerns. The Galveston branch of the organization performed valuable financial functions for Texas people. R. & D. G. Mills found it necessary to provide their numerous customers with some form of indebtedness in order to facilitate business transactions but state law prohibited the issue of any bill, promissory note, or other paper to circulate as money. A creative and lawful alternative was required.

At this time the Northern Bank of Mississippi at Holly Springs, a wildcat institution, had large amounts of paper money in circulation. Its paper was rejected everywhere. In order to provide some evidence of indebtedness to customers, the firm of R. & D. G. Mills of Galveston took these notes, endorsed them, and placed them in circulation at Galveston. With the endorsement of the reliable firm of R. & D. G. Mills, these banknotes were in demand everywhere. 'Mills money', as it was called, became the recognized currency and was considered equivalent to gold. Estimates of the amount of this type of money placed in circulation vary widely from $40,000 to $300,000. The firm of R. & D. G. Mills had not violated the laws of Texas prohibiting the issue of paper money. At most, they had merely re-issued banknotes that had been issued originally by the bank at Holly Springs. The Galveston firm was charged by the state government with violation of the law but the Supreme Court held in 1859 that this statute applied only to corporations such as the Dutch East India Company and that since the statute used the word "company", it was not intended to apply to a partnership like R. & D. G. Mills of Galveston. Thus the practice of re-issuing these banknotes was upheld.

In 1854, two additional important financial institutions started in Texas. In this year, B. A. Shepherd of Houston sold his interest in a mercantile partnership with A. J. Burke to open his own banking concern. We may credit Shepherd for being the first man to engage exclusively in banking in Texas. In 1857, his letterhead bore the words, "B. A. Shepherd, Exchange and Collection Office, Houston, Texas."

Ball, Hutchings & Company of Galveston was also established in 1854. This firm was a partnership consisting of John Sealy, John H. Hutchings and George Ball. The firm sold boots and shoes, hairpins, scissors, dry goods and other merchandise. In 1858 they advertised in a Galveston newspaper that they were "Wholesale Dealers in General Merchandise, Cotton Factors, and Commission Merchants." Ball, Hutchings & Company were the successors of the firm of Hutchings, Sealy & Simpson established at Sabine Pass on May 22, 1848. They were a firm of receiving, forwarding and commission merchants who also engaged in the general mercantile business and made liberal advances on consignments of produce to them. This firm still functions in Galveston today as the private bank of Hutchings, Sealy & Co. After the death of Samuel M.

Williams in 1858, the good will of the Commercial and Agricultural Bank was taken over by Ball, Hutchings & Company.

The prestigious firm continued through the Civil War and is in operation today as Hutchings, Sealy and Company, Bankers. Mr. Sealy Hutchings and Mr. George Ball, sons of the founders, still conduct the business. This private bank is the only banking institution that has functioned continuously throughout the entire financial history of Texas. While this old bank has continued to function under substantially the same type of organization with which it was created over seventy-five years ago, it has always adapted itself to serve the particular commercial and personal needs of the island community. It is an outstanding illustration of the genuine service that may be rendered any community by a private bank when the institution is conservatively managed.

The foundation of modern banking in Texas was laid at the close of the Civil War. While the origins of our banking system may be traced back to the period of the Republic of Texas, modern banking methods made only slight growth in the days following the war. During the war, the economic life of Texas people was closely allied with the Confederate cause and the monetary fiasco of that unfortunate government. Texas experienced the economic consequences which were visited upon the southern states during the war and Reconstruction. Approximately 605,000 people dwelt in this territory and the taxable value of all kinds of property, including slaves, was slightly less than $295,000,000. Texans suffered the evils of monetary inflation that characterized the war policies of the Confederate government, which resulted in a depreciating money, rising prices, wild speculation, profiteering and ultimate repudiation with the fall of the Confederacy. Although Texas didn't suffer any major land invasion by the Union and Texans were generally free to follow their usual agricultural pursuits, they nonetheless suffered numerous economic ills as the war progressed.

In Texas, as in other states of the south, Confederate treasury notes and bonds, notes of southern banks, obligations of southern states and cities, as well as corporate and individual paper flooded the state. Moreover Texas contributed to the financial debacle through the issue of city, county, and state warrants, which added to the tremendous volume of currency in circulation. The volume of state treasury notes outstanding at the close of the war was $2,068,998. The Texas Legislature cooperated faithfully with the Confederate government in its attempt to maintain the currency.

In addition to treasury notes, individual, railroad and corporation obligations were used as money in this state. Although Ball, Hutchings & Company, successors of the Commercial and Agricultural Bank at Galveston, R. & D. G. Mills of Galveston, T. W. House and the B. A. Shepherd Exchange and Collection Office at Houston continued to function as private bankers through the war period, there were no banks of issue in the state during the Civil War. The Commercial and Agricultural Bank which functioned between 1847 and 1858 was the only bank of issue in the state prior to the close of the war.

As a result of the confusion in the currency, a number of people considered it necessary to issue a local currency to meet the social demands in their respective communities. In the village of Fort Worth, for instance, an instrument known as a 'shinplaster' appeared in 1862. This was a simple written statement that "$2.50 in Confederate Notes or State Treasury Warrants will be paid when $20 is presented." It was signed by Chief Justice S. Terry and by G. Nance, County Clerk of Tarrant County. A similar case reached the Supreme Court of Texas in 1862, when an instrument in the following language was adjudicated by the court: "Mr. J. M. Luckey: Pay to bearer one dollar in currency, when twenty dollars are presented. F. M. Bates, Weatherford, Texas. February 24, 1862."

Numerous similar bills circulated freely throughout Weatherford. These bills appeared in printed form but were not engraved. And although they helped to satisfy the growing demand for more money, they further contributed to the ultimate ruin of the Confederate currency system. This type of money was illegal in Texas yet it persisted in several towns. The state did not contribute as freely to the volume of Confederate currency as did other southern states. The Texas Legislature, however, faithfully enforced the constitutional direction to prohibit chartered banks and the issue of bank paper to circulate as money. Thus Texas anticipated the policy of the United States in prohibiting the circulation of state banknotes after 1866.

The use of Confederate currency caused many legal complications in Texas after the close of the war. Numerous business transactions occurred during the war whereupon final settlement was not made until after the fall of the Confederacy. Lands, for instance, were frequently sold on installment plans and after the war, the question was presented: "In what kind of currency shall this contract be fulfilled?" In general, the Texas courts refused to recognize the Confederate currency after the war ended and in some cases held contracts void for uncertainty. Although executed contracts were not disturbed, executory contracts were regarded as illegal and unenforceable. The courts in Texas followed the common law rule of keeping hands-off illegal contracts. This situation caused numerous embarrassing conditions in the commercial life of the state.

The National Bank Act of 1863 and the minimum $50,000 capital requirement that it imposed on would-be national banks in the United States, combined with the prohibition of state banks in Texas, significantly spurred the growth of private banks in this state. In 1865 and 1866, after the close of the Civil War, a mere four national banks were chartered in Texas under the National Bank Act of 1863. Two of these institutions were located in Galveston, one at Houston, and one in San Antonio. The scarcity of capital in post-war Texas made it difficult to raise the necessary $50,000 to organize a national bank. Hence, the private bank proved to be the outlet for the development of a financial system. Because of these factors, the period of growth between the Panic of 1873 and the Panic of 1893 may well be designated as "The Reign of the Private Banker in Texas."

By 1868 there were at least fifteen private bankers operating in Texas. According to the *Texas Almanac* for 1867 and 1869, these banks were as follows:

Fig. 1

Location	Firm Name	NY Correspondent
Austin	Raymond & Swisher	J.H. Brower & Co.
Belton	Chamberlain & Flint	J.H. Brower & Co.
Brenham	Bassett & Bassett	J.H. Brower & Co.
Galveston	Butler, George	Duncan Sherman & Co
Galveston	Hewitt, Swisher & Co.	R. Atkinson & Co.
Galveston	McMahan & Gilbert	National Park Bank
Galveston	W. H. Nichols & Co.	Importers & Traders National Bank
Galveston	W. B. Sorley & Co.	Duncan Sherman & Co.
Galveston	Ball, Hutchings & Co.	Hopkins, Swight & Trowbridge
Houston	B. A. Shepherd & Co.	J.H. Brower & Co.
Houston	R. P. Pulliam & Co.	S.M. Swenson & Co.
San Antonio	A. W. Bennett	J.H. Brower & Co.
San Antonio	Houston Insurance Co.	Northrup & Chick
Waco	Flint & Chamberlain	J.H. Brower & Co.

These private bankers made no official reports to any supervising agency and were totally unregulated. Some of them engaged in the cotton commission business and collections were one of their chief services. We find Raymond & Swisher of Austin advertising themselves as "Bankers and Exchange Dealers." They announced that they were prepared to make "collections in all accessible points in Texas" and that proceeds were "promptly remitted." Hewitt, Swisher & Company of Galveston advertised themselves as "Cotton Factors, Commission Merchants and Exchange Dealers." It appears that banking was largely a sideline with this firm. There were other cotton factors that engaged in the performance of banking functions in connection with the cotton commission business, although they were not listed as bankers. The firm of T. H. McMahan & Company, for instance, advertised as "General Commission Merchants and Dealers in Domestic and Foreign Exchange." Thomas H. McMahan of this company was one of Texas's great business leaders following the Civil War. He was also associated with the banking firm of McMahan & Gilbert at Galveston. He went on to serve as president of the first bank to be organized in Texas under the National Bank Act of 1863, the First National Bank organized at Galveston, September 22, 1865.

Private banking services during the Reconstruction period in Texas were performed largely in connection with the cotton export business in Galveston. The commercial supremacy of this thriving city attracted numerous financial concerns to Galveston. For instance, J. S. and J. B. Sydnor, who conducted an auction business in Houston, removed to Galveston in 1867 and announced that they were prepared to make liberal advances on consignments of all kinds of merchandise. Similarly, Burns & Lee were engaged as "wholesale dealers in foreign and domestic exchange." Likewise, Felder & Shipman, cotton and wool factors, and Baker, Walker & Company, also of Galveston, announced that they were prepared to make "liberal cash advancements on consignment for sale or shipment." Flint & Chamberlin of Waco announced that they gave special attention to collections, collected paper payable in Waco with exchange and remitted promptly on the day of payment. They mentioned Ball, Hutchings & Company of Galveston, the First National Bank of Houston and banks in New Orleans and New York as their correspondents. Similarly, Haswell & Son advertised as receiving, forwarding and commission merchants, who made liberal advances on all consignments. In 1867, Wheelock, Findley & Ball, commission merchants, announced that their terms were net cash, in accordance with present business usage both in Europe and this country.

During the early years of Reconstruction, the Galveston cotton commission merchants continued their practices of making advances to cotton growers. These firms which were exporting cotton found it necessary, in the absence of adequate banking facilities, to perform certain banking functions for their customers. As the demand for banking facilities grew, the commission men set up their own private banks. Information is not available regarding the profits earned by these bankers but we are led to believe that their earnings were quite satisfactory since so many individuals were attracted to the business.

The Texas Legislature authorized the incorporation of state-chartered banks under the Constitution of 1869. Apparently the only limitations on the capital that could be authorized were the imagination of the promoters and the conservatism of the Legislature. To charter a bank by a special act of the Legislature was a surmountable task but raising the necessary capital in Texas in the early 1870s was an entirely different problem. Capital was scarce in Texas during this period. The Legislature generally provided a minimum capital varying from $25,000 to $250,000 according to the population of the city in which the bank was to be organized. Because of the economic conditions which were present in Texas in the early 1870s and the monetary situation which prevailed throughout the United States just prior to the panic of 1873, little specie was available for investment in these bank stocks. The Legislature attempted to provide the machinery under which the people could build their own banking system. It scrupulously avoided the unfortunate experiences of other states in voting state bond issues to provide the capital for banks. But there was apparently little desire to extend the credit of the state to any scheme to subsidize banks. Although state-chartered banks were legal, the capital required was prohibitive and gave rise to an even larger number of private banks.

In 1869, the Houston Insurance Company, which conducted both an insurance and a banking business, declared a dividend of $10 per share on their $250,000 capital. This concern was considered one of the most substantial financial companies in the south. In 1870, the City Bank of Houston was chartered by the state to take over the banking portion of the business of the Houston Insurance Company. This bank did a thriving business from its beginning. In 1871, it was reported to have declared a dividend of 20 percent.

During the year 1869, twenty additional private banks were opened in Texas. These institutions were located in Austin, Belton, Brownsville, Bryan, Corpus Christi, Dallas, Galveston, Houston, Indianola, Jefferson, Lavaca, McKinney, Nacogdoches, San Antonio, and Waco. The cities of Austin and San Antonio each received three new bankers. Jefferson got two and each of the remaining towns each welcomed one additional private bank. All these firms were partnerships with the exception of D. A. Wray of Brownsville, James Arbuckle of Jefferson, and J. S. Lockwood of San Antonio. Each of these new firms had New York correspondents. By the close of 1869, it is estimated that there were at least thirty-five private banks in operation in Texas. All of these banks engaged in making collections in various parts of the state. They received deposits and made loans and discounts but were not permitted to issue circulating notes.

Some of the men behind these new private banks had already proven themselves as experienced and responsible bankers. A few had held posts at banks outside of Texas. One fine example is George W. Jackson, of the firm of Fort & Jackson at Waco, who had been cashier of the First National Bank of Gallipolis, Ohio. The partnership was organized by

William A. Fort, a native of Alabama who came to Texas in 1854, and Mr. Jackson of Ohio. The firm had connections in Cincinnati, New Orleans and New York City. In 1874, the partnership was incorporated as the Waco National Bank, with Mr. Fort as president and Mr. Jackson as cashier. This case illustrates the evolution of many private banks, which subsequently incorporated as national banks in Texas.

The history of banking in Texas is riddled with tales of creative pioneer banking practices. One such example is that of Faultin and Schreiner. In December of 1869, Charles Schreiner of the village of Kerrville and August Faultin of Comfort opened a mercantile concern at Kerrville, in a small building sixteen by eighteen feet in size. Since there were no banks in that section of the state, Faultin and Schreiner were frequently called upon to perform numerous banking functions in connection with their store. The cattlemen in the community usually received gold and silver for their stock. Many of these coins were Spanish doubloons, which were gold coins varying in value from five dollars to sixteen dollars. Most of these cattlemen turned their coins over to the store for safekeeping and simply wrote an order to Faultin and Schreiner to pay their bills owed to merchants throughout the village. As the firm had no safe, the coins were deposited in a box placed underneath some loose boards in the floor. A barrel of salt and some boxes were then placed over the plank. Other boxes of specie were secreted to the homes of the partners and other boxes stored in unsuspected places. Although the store was robbed frequently, the money was never placed in a safe and Faultin & Schreiner always paid specie on demand. Thus originated a unique business which survives to this day as the Chas. Schreiner Bank at Kerrville. The Schreiner bank has been very influential in promoting the thriving mohair industry in that region.

During the year 1870, eight more private banks opened for business in communities across Texas. Two were located in the town of Calvert, two in Galveston, two at Jefferson, one in Marshall and one at Sherman. By the close of 1870, there were approximately forty-three private banks operating in the state. Some of these firms, however, were not devoted solely to banking and would not be described as banks by today's standards. In many cases, their banking functions were merely incidental to some other primary business, such as real estate or insurance.

The following year, Texans had eight new private banks with whom they could conduct business. By the close of 1871, approximately fifty private banks were in operation. There were also five national banks and one state bank in operation. During 1872, thirty-two additional private banks were added to the banking facilities of the state, while four institutions were dissolved, leaving a net addition of twenty-seven private banks. Approximately seventy-seven private bankers were thus engaged in banking at the end of this year.

The year 1872 also marked the organization of a banking partnership in Fort Worth known as Tidball and Wilson. In July of 1873, Khleber Miller Van Zandt, a Civil War veteran and promising merchant at Fort Worth who had been trained for the law, purchased Mr. Wilson's interest in the firm. Thus the new bank of Tidball, Van Zandt & Company was organized. J. Peter Smith and Major J. J. Jarvis, who were both lawyers, and Thomas A. Tidball were the other members of this firm. Mr. Van Zandt and Mr. Tidball were the active partners in charge of the work and employed one bookkeeper. They had capital of only $10,000 and, in the words of Major Van Zandt, "a lot of courage." This private bank continued until January 1884, in a small building twenty-five by thirty feet on Weatherford Street in Fort Worth.

Fort Worth in the 1870s was a thriving village of one thousand people. It was located at the juncture of two great cattle trails, the Baxter Springs and the Chisholm Trail, over which thousands of cattle were driven to Abilene, Kansas, the primary railroad terminal for shipping cattle to the slaughterhouses in Chicago. Tidball, Van Zandt & Company served the credit needs of the many cattlemen. Money was scarce in Fort Worth at the time and a gold coin always attracted attention.

Major Van Zandt relates how an outfit of cattle drovers camped one night southwest of the city, purchased a liberal supply of provisions at a store and paid for the articles with a glistening twenty dollar gold piece. The overjoyed storekeeper rode to town and paid his family physician. The physician then rushed across the street to pay his overdue grocery bill. The valuable coin chased about the village during the day, paid over $200 in debts and in the evening came back to the original storekeeper in payment of some hay he had previously sold. Then it was deposited in the bank for safekeeping, where it served as gold reserve for several days. This incident convinced the Major Van Zandt of the value of sound money and safe banks.

K. M. Van Zandt was also instrumental in persuading the Texas & Pacific Railroad to build west through Fort Worth and in July of 1876, the shriek of the locomotive was heard for the first time in this thriving village. In March 1884, the Fort Worth National Bank with a capital of $30,000 succeeded the private bank of Tidball, Van Zandt & Company with Mr. Van Zandt as president. Today, at the age of ninety-three years, this honorable banker may be found at his desk in the Fort Worth National Bank every day, where he continues to serve as active president, a position he has held for over forty-six years. The son of a pioneer statesman of the Republic of Texas, he has lived through the entire history of Texas banking, and personifies all that is good in our banking system.

At the close of 1873, there were approximately eighty-six private banks operating in Texas. The true number of banks in operation, however, depends largely on one's definition of the term 'bank.' Since banking was frequently combined with mercantile, commission, real estate and brokerage concerns, confusion naturally resulted in the estimates of the total number of private banks in the state. The Panic of 1873, which wreaked financial havoc throughout the northeast, appears to have affected Texas banking only slightly. The Texas frontier was simply too far removed from the more complicated business organizations of the industrial eastern U.S. to feel serious effects from this depression. No official estimates of the number of private banks appeared until 1875. At that time, the report of the United States Commissioner of Internal Revenue tallied ninety-five private banks in Texas. By the close of Reconstruction, private banking had made considerable progress in this state.

The following table, compiled from announcements in the *Bankers Magazine* and other sources, represents a reasonably accurate estimate of the number of private bankers in Texas for the years 1868 – 1893.

PRIVATE BANKS IN TEXAS 1868 – 1893

Fig. 2

Year	Banks	Year	Banks
1868	15	1881	107
1869	20	1882	123
1870	43	1883	123
1871	50	1884	122
1872	77	1885	116
1873	86	1886	112
1874	104	1887	122
1875	95	1888	130
1876	89	1889	138
1877	94	1890	148
1878	85	1891	145
1879	88	1892	127
1880	87	1893	133

As stated previously, it was not always possible to determine when a business institution was a bank, and when it was a commission firm or a mercantile establishment. Only meager information is available concerning the capital of these banks. Since these institutions were not subject to inspection, they seldom furnished a financial statement. Each bank was afraid to give out information for fear it would be used against it by competitors. Banking had not reached the stage where financial information was regarded as a matter of public concern.

A number of the more ambitious bankers did announce the amount of their capital, although information is not available as to how much of this amount was actually paid up. The announced capital ranged from $20,000 to $75,000. Among the larger private banks in the 1880s were the Fort Worth Stock Yards Bank, with an announced capital of $250,000. The Bank of Van Alstyne claimed a capital of $300,000. The City Savings Bank of Waco, The Texas Loan and Trust Company of San Marcos, and the Merchants Exchange Bank of El Paso each announced a capital of $100,000. The San Antonio Loan and Trust Company claimed a capital of $1,000,000 in 1892. The Bank of Goliad also claimed a $1,000,000 capital.

While the Panic of 1893 did not ruin the private banks in Texas, a number of them indeed failed. The process of reorganization of these institutions into national banks continued well into the twentieth century. While new private banks were being opened, the incidence of closure or conversion to national banks was far more prevalent. Each monthly issue of the *Banker's Magazine* contained announcements of new Texas banks during the late 1890s, but more frequently notices were made regarding banking firms that had dissolved. Nonetheless, the process of private bank promotion which enjoyed such widespread popularity during the previous two decades persisted through the 1890s and into the twentieth century, until the restoration of the state banking system in 1905.

According to the best figures available, Texas had the following number of private bankers during the years indicated. (see Figure 6)

Fig. 3

PRIVATE BANKERS IN TEXAS, 1894 – 1905

Year	Number of Banks
1894	128
1895	131
1896	153
1897	146
1898	165
1899	187
1900	190
1901	195
1902	168
1903	183
1904	184
1905	197

The figures during the first six years above are the estimates of Dr. George E. Barnett, which were based on *The Banker's Almanac and Register*. The figures from 1900 to 1905 are based on the reports of the National Monetary Commission. Since private banks made no official reports, little reliable information concerning the condition of these private banks is available. Even the United States Comptroller of the Currency was able to gather only meager information concerning the private banks in Texas. This scarcity of information was likely due to a combination of causes, among them being the inadequate transportation facilities in the state, the sheer size of the state, its location far removed from the commercial life of the northeast and the independent spirit of the Texas pioneer banker, who refused to be regulated or to provide information for governmental authorities. Even today, the few remaining private bankers insist that their financial affairs are strictly private.

The financial reports of a very limited number of private banks in Texas, which were published by the United States Comptroller of the Currency, throw considerable light on the condition of these institutions. The following table reveals the financial tendencies of those private banks which reported their condition to the Comptroller:

Fig. 4

TEXAS PRIVATE BANKS, 1894 – 1928

Year	Banks Reporting	Total Resources	Total Deposits	Total Capital Surplus & Undivided Profits
1894	20	$6,228,000	$2,877,000	$3,085,000
1899	33	$6,703,000	$2,849,000	$1,468,000
1904	12	$11,550,000	$7,355,000	$3,856,000
1909	60	$15,893,000	$9,276,000	$2,956,000
1914	36	$4,692,000	$2,351,000	$1,326,000
1919	38	$8,291,000	$3,815,000	$1,802,000
1924	18	$3,248,000	$2,236,000	$771,000
1928	14	$8,407,000	$6,890,000	$1,146,000

Figure 4 indicates that the private banks carried on an extensive banking business in Texas at the turn of the century, especially considering that the figures represent only a small percentage of existing banks. Less than 25 percent submitted their financial statements to the Comptroller. The principal items on the combined balance sheet of the reporting banks extended into millions of dollars. For the twelve years prior to the restoration of the state banking system, the average loans and discounts of these institutions exceeded four million dollars each year.

Private bank regulation was proposed while the Legislature was enacting the State Banking Law of 1905. This proposal prompted stiff opposition from the private bankers throughout the state and the potential unconstitutionality of the proposed law immediately sparked discussion by lawyers on both sides of the issue. On January 31, 1905, fifty private bankers attended a public hearing in Austin held by the House Committee on Private Corporations. As one might expect, they voiced strong opposition to the proposed law requiring state supervision of their institutions.

T. W. Gregory of Austin appeared as attorney for the private bankers. He made a vigorous and emotional argument against the proposal. Mr. Gregory's argument, while not impressive in all respects, represented the point of view of the private bankers at that time. He argued that honesty cannot be legislated into bankers, be they national, state or private bankers. He continued:

> The cry of the widow has been heard in every part of the land notwithstanding the fine national banks... I am here to speak for the men who with their fathers and grandfathers have borne the burdens of the financial system of the state for sixty years, long before there were any national banks ... men who have conducted this business honorably and honestly and who have maintained the credit of the state through every crisis,

even through war and panic. They are asking for
nothing whatever, but to be let alone, the right to
do those things which their fathers did.

He further argued that the proposed state banks would receive
a number of special privileges, such as limited liability on
stockholders, while the private bankers were subject to unlimited liability. He said that it was unfair to restrict the loans of
private banks while subjecting them to inspection and publicity, since they received of these special privileges. He pointed
to the limitation on loans of national banks and many state
banks to 10 percent of their capital, while private bankers with
their freedom from regulation were able to serve their communities without being hampered by such restrictions.

Mr. Gregory cited as an example of the valuable service
rendered by private bankers, the case of a private bank in a
west Texas town of 6,000 people. The bank had loaned annually $100,000 to an oil mill, $60,000 to a flour mill and $100,000
to cotton exporters. He neglected to discuss the soundness of
making these large loans to a so few borrowers. He probably
did not realize that such loans are one of the principal causes
of bank failures. He also referred to a case where a number of
national banks, in cooperation, had arranged to carry 10,000
bales of cotton for the cotton growers, while at the same time
a private banker was financing 40,000 bales of cotton through
a million dollar loan — a thing that no national bank could do.
He neglected, however, to discuss the safety of depositor's
money in national banks versus private bank in case of a
sudden drop in the cotton market. This representative of the
private bankers contended that they were able to compete
with the big national banks because of their immunity from
sworn reports. He argued that the proposal to regulate private
banks was equivalent to driving them out of business.

In answer to questions concerning the safety of these institutions, Mr. Gregory declared that the unlimited liability on
private bankers forced them to be far more careful with funds
than the incorporated banks which have only a few thousand

dollars at stake. It was also contended that the depositor in a private bank was protected by a statute prohibiting the acceptance of deposits when the owner knows the bank to be insolvent. After declaring that not a single depositor in the Texas private banks was demanding regulation, Mr. Gregory concluded his oratorical effort be referring to the fountainhead of democracy, Thomas Jefferson, who believed that every individual has a right to earn his living in any business he may select and that private individuals shall not be driven out business by corporations.

It is hard to conceive of a more distorted analysis of the functions of a private bank. However, this argument was characteristic of the influences that have historically shaped the banking policies in our state. Texas politicians have always turned to lawyers and emotional spellbinders for inspiration in legislating on financial affairs, rather than to the cold logic of conservative bankers and the impartial analysis of facts by trained economists. That policy on the part of the state has cursed financial legislation in Texas to this very day.

While the state bank legislation of 1905 did not molest the private bankers, the address of Mr. Gregory and the ensuing discussion proved to be the swan song of the private bank system in Texas. With the restoration of the state bank system, the influence and prestige of private bankers rapidly declined. Several Commissioners of Insurance and Banking recommended that the supervisory power of the state be extended to the private banks. Such suggestions were made officially in 1909, 1912, and 1919. It appears, however, that state officials had their hands full in supervising the state banks adequately without adding these additional duties. The private bankers successfully resisted control by the state until 1923, when the Legislature enacted a law declaring it to be "the policy of the State that no additional private banking institutions or business shall be organized or established." This law, as amended in 1925, permitted existing private banks to continue but prohibited the organization of new private banks. The effect was to prohibit the extension of the private banking system in Texas.

While the private bank is a dying institution in the state, a number of them still persist with remarkable tenacity. Moreover, some of the remaining private banks are among the state's most noted institutions and have rendered a long period of faithful service. The private banker played has indeed left his mark on the historical development of banking in Texas.

THE SAGA OF STATE BANKS

The money lenders and the semi-mercantile bank organizations of antebellum Texas were succeeded by private bankers, and a small number of state and national banks. To a large extent, the private bankers dominated commercial life in Texas until after 1893. The growth of the private bank system was simultaneous with the development of national banks in the state beginning in 1865, since state-chartered banks were prohibited. There were no regular banking houses outside of Galveston and Houston, until after the Civil War. A few merchants in Austin, Dallas, San Antonio and Waco carried on an exchange business as a convenience for their customers in the dry goods, grocery and general merchandise trades.

While the State Constitutions of 1861 and 1866 had prohibited the organization of corporations with banking powers, there appears to have been strong sentiment among the people for the creation of a state banking system. The Constitution of 1869, enforced by the Reconstruction government, accordingly omitted the language of previous constitutions prohibiting the incorporation of banks. The framers of this constitution attempted to solve the monetary heresies which had blighted Texas since 1836, by providing that "in no case shall the Legislature have power to issue treasury warrants, treasury notes, or paper of any description intended to circulate as money." The demand for banking facilities and the allowance made by the new constitution led to the establishment of the first state banking system in 1870. In total, forty-eight institutions were chartered by the Reconstruction government. Of these forty-eight, only eighteen institutions are known to have actually opened for business.

Between 1870 and 1873, inclusive, a large number of state banks were created by special charter. In the absence of a general banking law, when a group of men desired to incorporate a state bank, they had to secure from the Legislature a special charter. In 1870, ten state banks were created in this manner under charters ranging from twenty to fifty years in duration. Of these ten original special charters granted, only three were ever used. Apparently, the other corporations were unable to raise the required to legally open for business.

In 1871, twenty additional state banks were incorporated by special legislative acts. Their authorized capital ranged from $30,000 to $5,000,000 depending largely on the imagination of the promoters and the graces of the Legislature. Apparently, obtaining the charter was relatively easy but raising the required capital in post-war Texas was not. In the following two years, an increasing number of state banks were chartered, yet a total of eight of these specially chartered state banks are known to have ever opened for business. These banks are shown below, in order of the dates of their respective charters.

Fig. 5

Bank Name	Location	Charter Date
Island City Savings Bank	Galveston	June 20, 1870
Texas Banking & Insurance Co.	Galveston	July 1, 1870
City Bank of Houston	Houston	July 21, 1870
State Central Bank of Waco	Waco	August 8, 1870
Citizens Bank of Navasota	Navasota	March 31, 1871
Galveston Bank & Trust Co.	Galveston	Dec. 2, 1871
City Bank of Sherman	Sherman	April 11, 1873
City Bank of Dallas	Dallas	May 31, 1873

Some of these banks had long and honorable careers but others, born during the rapid descent into the Panic of 1873, did not. The Island City Savings Bank was the first state bank in Texas to actually open its doors for business. It flourished in Galveston for a period of fifteen years and failed on January 25, 1885. A reorganization occurred and a new bank opened in the same building on March 20, 1885 as its successor. The new institution received the assets of the old bank, used the seal of the former and claimed to operate under the same charter. In a suit filed by a depositor of the old bank, the succeeding institution was held liable for the debts of the old bank on the grounds that it was merely a continuation of the Island City Savings Bank. In 1891, a run occurred on this bank but it was successfully met.

The Texas Banking & Insurance Company had a capital of $150,000 and was engaged in a thriving banking business in Galveston in 1872. In 1889, it was succeeded by the Galveston National Bank. The State Central Bank of Waco and Citizens Bank of Navasota did not open for business until 1875. Little is known of their operations.

The City Bank of Houston was chartered to take over the banking portion of the Houston Insurance Company. This bank did a thriving business with its $250,000 capital and on October 31, 1871 declared a 20 percent dividend. The capital was soon increased to $500,000 although it appears this figure was grossly inflated. While it was a state bank, the City Bank of Houston made no financial reports to the state. According to its charter, this institution was organized "for the purpose of transacting a general banking and exchange business with power to receive money and other valuables to keep for depositors, to issue certificates or bills of exchange, loan money and discount negotiable paper."

This institution maintained commercial relations with the Texas Banking and Insurance Company of Galveston, the First National Bank of Houston, C. R. Johns & Co. of Austin and others. The Continental National Bank of New York customarily discounted the paper of the City Bank of Houston. In 1885, this institution engaged in advertising campaign to bolster its failing credit. The daily newspapers of Houston, the city directory and conspicuous signboards were used to call attention to this bank and attract new depositors. A large signboard in front of the bank bore the words, "Capital $500,000." In a lawsuit in which the institution became involved, it came to light that the bank had been hopelessly insolvent since September 20, 1885. The directors were held personally liable to depositors because of the false advertising. After more than fifteen years of service, it passed into the hands of a receiver in January 1886.

The Galveston Bank & Trust Company, chartered December 2, 1871, was the first state bank in Texas with trust powers. Henry Rosenberg, whose name is a household word in Galveston because of his generous benefactions to that city, was the first president and moving spirit of this bank. Isadore Dyer, Albert Fall, John Sealy, and J. H. Hutchings were the other prominent financiers identified with the promotion of this institution. This bank was authorized to receive deposits, act as administrator, guardian and as receiver. It commenced business in the latter part of 1875 with a capital of $250,000 and continued to function until 1882, when it liquidated voluntarily. This bank represented a significant contribution to Texas banking by an immigrant Texan. Immediately, after the liquidation of the Galveston Bank & Trust Company, Mr. Rosenberg purchased the building and opened a private bank, which he conducted under the name of "H. Rosenberg, Banker" until his death in 1893.

Mr. Rosenberg, a native of Switzerland, landed at Galveston in February 1843 at the age of nineteen years and became a clerk in a dry goods store. He soon purchased the store and conducted it for many years. This store grew into one of the leading dry goods concerns in the south by 1859 and by the 1880s Mr. Rosenberg became one of Texas's wealthiest men. He served as director in several banks, as president of the Gulf, Colorado & Santa Fe Railway, as Switzerland's consul in Galveston and in many other public positions. His magnificent gifts to his adopted city, which include a monument to the heroes of the Texas Revolution, a high school building, a YMCA building, a church, and the wonderful Rosenberg Library, reveal the generous character of the man who gave Texas a fine example of business leadership. As Samuel May Williams was Texas's leading banker and businessman of the 1840s and 1850s, so was Henry Rosenberg the outstanding banker and leader of commerce in the 1870s and 1880s. Both were adopted sons of Texas.

The City Bank of Sherman opened in 1873 at Sherman and was functioning as late as December 1885. Its announced capital

capital was $200,000, although it is not known whether this figure represented real capital. The institution made no reports to the state but its officers were announced in *Bankers Magazine*, and it is known to have handled drafts on the City Bank of Houston.

Also organized in 1873, the City Bank of Dallas was authorized by its fifty-year charter "to deal in foreign and domestic exchange, banknotes, coin, bullion, etc., to buy and sell stock, scrip and bonds, to make advances on wool, cotton, stock, grain, and other valuable articles, to loan money and to perform all acts incident to a general banking business." Its first financial statement to the Secretary of State was filed in January 1874. By 1879, its total assets exceeded $181,000. In 1880 this bank was converted into the City National Bank of Dallas, which later merged with the American Exchange National Bank. This merger resulted in the present First National Bank in Dallas.

An attempt was made to set up branches of some Texas banks in the early 1870s. The Bank of Texas, incorporated in 1871, was to be located at Austin and had "authority to place an agency in any town in the state, or in any other locality." Similarly, the Merchants and Planters Savings Bank of Texas, chartered at Austin the same year, was authorized "to establish such and as many branch offices in this State or in other States, as its directors shall provide." Likewise, the Banking, Insurance and Mutual Aid Association of Texas, and the Home Insurance and Trust Company, located at Austin and Galveston respectively, in 1871 were authorized to establish branches. All of these institutions were unsuccessful in raising the necessary capital and they failed to open for business. The City Bank of Sherman was authorized to establish branches, but none were located.

A law providing for the incorporation of savings banks under general regulations was enacted in 1871, but it did not become effective for constitutional reasons until after it was amended in 1874. Thereafter state banks in Texas were chartered by the Secretary of State under the general banking law of

April 23, 1874. There were at least sixteen banks chartered under the general bank act of 1874 that never opened. Ten state banks were brought into existence under the new law, however, as shown below.

Fig. 6

BANK NAME	LOCATION	DATE OF CHARTER	CAPITAL
Fannin County Bank	Bonham	January 27, 1874	$50,000
Red River County Bank	Clarksville	September 12, 1874	$10,000
Merchants & Planters Bank	Sherman	September 28, 1872	$150,000
Farmers & Merchants Bank	Paris	May 16, 1874	$250,000
Paris Exchange Bank	Paris	January 28, 1875	$300,000
Exchange Bank of Dallas	Dallas	October 11, 1875	$40,000
State Savings Bank of Dallas	Dallas	December 1875	$50,000
Drovers & Planters Bank	Denison	1876	———
Merchants & Planters Bank	Denison	———	———
Citizens Savings Bank	Jefferson	———	———

Little is known about the Drovers & Planters Bank of Denison. It made a semi-annual report on January 28, 1876. About that date, it was merged with the Merchants & Planters Bank of Denison and the combined institution failed in 1878. The Citizens Savings Bank of Jefferson made no official reports to the state, although it was reputed to have raised a capital of $50,000 and to have conducted a general banking business.

The Fannin County Bank at Bonham was a successor of the firm of J. R. Russell & Company, private bankers. On October 3, 1898, this bank was converted into the Fannin County National

Bank with a capital of $100,000. It continued as a national bank until October 2, 1918, when its charter expired and a new state bank was organized under Texas law as its successor. The Red River County Bank at Clarksville continued under an exceptionally conservative management until 1894, when it became a national bank.

The Merchants and Planters Bank of Sherman was converted into a national bank, known by the same name, in May 1884. Its capital was $600,000. Tom Randolph, who had entered the bank's employ as a young man in 1872, continued as cashier of the new institution and Judge C. C. Binkley served as president until his death in 1886. Mr. Randolph was then promoted to the presidency, which position he held until his death in 1918. C. B. Dorchester, who entered the employ of the bank on November 5, 1875 at the age of nineteen years became cashier on January 1, 1876. In January 1918, Mr. Dorchester became the institution's third president, a position he holds today. This was one of the rare banks that built for permanency in a time when wildcat banking blighted the country.

The Farmers and Merchants Bank at Paris had over $231,000 in total assets at the close of 1878. By 1892, its total assets exceeded $551,000. The institution had a long career of service but ultimately failed in March 1896.

The Exchange Bank of Dallas had quite a complex history. It began in 1871, when W. H. Gaston and A. C. Camp started a semi-banking and brokerage business in Dallas. Shortly thereafter, Mr. Camp retired and a new partnership, Gaston & Thomas, was formed. According to legend, these men used a dry goods box for a counter and their pockets served as safes. In 1881, they acquired control of the Exchange Bank of Dallas. On January 31, 1887 the bank was liquidated and was succeeded by the National Exchange Bank. Ten years later, this institution absorbed the Mercantile National Bank of Dallas and in 1900 it absorbed the National Bank of Dallas. In 1905, the National Exchange Bank merged with the American National Bank, capital increased to $1,000,000, and the American Exchange National Bank was born. Here is a Texas institution that has evolved from a private bank, to a state bank and finally a national bank. Today it is one of the largest banks in the entire south, the First National Bank in Dallas.

The legislative pendulum swung against state banks a mere two years after the 1874 general banking act generally permitted state-chartered banks. The Texas Constitution of 1876 once again prohibited the state from chartering banks and this remained the law of the land for more than a quarter of a century, giving rise to more private and national banks.

These state banks had rendered a valuable service to the people of Texas during the last quarter of the nineteenth century. Official reports indicate that their deposits were relatively large. They made extensive loans and usually kept a large cash reserve. While the law made no rules for the conduct of the banking business, and the state exercised little supervision over them, their extensive reports indicate conservative management. Since interest rates were not restricted by law at this time, these banks were permitted to charge such interest rates as they saw fit. Competition for business was the leading influence which determined interest rates.

These institutions, scattered throughout the expanse of Texas, flourished before the days of adding machines, comptometers, typewriters, electric lights and other modern banking conveniences. Their books were kept and balances written in the careful hand of the bookkeepers. In this bygone era, banking was a personal matter between the banker and his customer. Loans were made largely on the basis of character and the necessities of the borrower were given serious consideration. The impersonal attitudes adopted by the modern twentieth-century banker in our large cities was not present in the 1870s and 1880s. The small-town banker knew each customer personally, knew his circumstances and frequently called him by his first name. Likewise, the bank's customers took the banker into their complete confidence. The ideals, services and policies followed by these bankers under the first state banking system in Texas provide valuable examples which more modern bankers might well imitate.

The notion that banking was a private business, in which the government must not interfere, died hard in Texas. The growing number of successful national banks indicated an increasing confidence in the principles of regulation by the government. The unique feature of the development of state control in Texas was the fact that a state banking system was adopted, dismantled and restored again. This prohibition of banks by constitutional means is also a fine example of the inadvisability of trying to solve current economic problems by inserting regulative and prohibitive clauses into the State Constitution. A constitution must be flexible enough to be adjusted to changing economic thought and the lives of the citizens whose lives it governs. The cause of the anti-bank faction triumphed in 1876, but changing industrial conditions and an advancing civilization demanded a well organized state banking system. Today, many people rightfully wonder why the pioneers of that day actually opposed state-chartered banks.

On August 14, 1905, the State of Texas reestablished its state banking system, which had been in a state of hibernation since 1876. The people had to depend on private banks and the national institutions for banking facilities during this period, with the exception of the eighteen state banks chartered by special legislative acts between 1870 and 1876. The restoration of the state banking system, however, was not accomplished without bitter political controversy.

As early as 1893, Governor J. S. Hogg recommended an amendment to the constitution to permit state banks. In 1902, the Democratic party in Texas incorporated a plank in its platform calling for an amendment to the constitution that would again permit the organization of state banks. The Twenty-eighth Legislature passed a joint resolution providing for such a constitutional amendment. Accordingly, it was submitted to the people in the election of November 1904 and won their approval. But the two leading political parties in this state continued to debate the banking issue although the people had already spoken. The Democrats endorsed the proposed amendment but the Republicans, not to be outdone in the making of political platforms, met at Fort Worth and declared: "We believe in the passage and vigorous enforcement of an adequate usury law, which will drive the usurer from our State, and we oppose any such change in the garnishment statutes, as would jeopardize the wage earner's salary....We denounce the proposed Constitutional amendment, for the imposition of additional taxation and the creation of State banks as an attempt to saddle a wild cat currency upon our people."

The Texas Bankers Association at their El Paso meeting in 1904 had passed a resolution requesting the Twenty-ninth Legislature to create a state banking system. They renewed their endorsement of the cause in 1905. This prominent and active banker's organization was regarded as one of the staunchest supporters of the state system.

The constitutional amendment had already been approved by the citizens of Texas and it was expected that the Twenty-Ninth Legislature, meeting in January 1905, would promptly create a banking system. It did not. Governor S. W. T. Lanham referred to the bank question in his message to the Legislature in these words: "Great care should also be devoted to the preparation and passage of any measure to make effective the amendment relating to the incorporation of state banks, to the end that the public may be duly protected."

Four months later, when the defeat of the bank bill seemed imminent, the Dallas *News* declared that the constitutional amendment was a mandate from the people to enact a bank law. A number of bank bills were introduced in the Legislature but it was Senator Thomas B. Love of Dallas who fathered the bill that ultimately became the law. Senator Love's bill proposed to regulate private banks as well as state banks and to create trust companies to operate under the same act. The portion of the bill that proposed to regulate private bankers met with defeat but the rest of Senator Love's bill was written into law. This new law which restored the state banking system was a comprehensive statute. It provided for the creation of banks of deposit and discount, savings banks and trust companies, by certificate from the Secretary of State.

The Texas State Bank Law of 1905 provided that any five or more persons, three of whom were residents of the state, might establish a bank of deposit, by complying with certain administrative requirements. The minimum capital for such banks was placed at $10,000 for banks located in towns of less than 2,500 people. In towns of 2,500 to 10,000 people, the minimum capital requirement was placed at $25,000. For institutions in cities of 10,000 to 20,000 people, the minimum capital was $50,000 and in cities of 20,000 or more inhabitants, the minimum capital was fixed at $100,000. These institutions were authorized to carry on the usual banking functions, such as receiving deposits, dealing in exchange and loaning money on real estate and personal property. The loans made by state banks on real estate were limited to not more than fifty percent of the "reasonable cash value" of the land and no institution was permitted to loan more than fifty percent of its funds on land. Branch banking was prohibited. The usual double liability on stock was provided in the constitutional provision. These state banks were required to maintain a cash reserve of ten percent of their demand deposits and twenty-five percent reserve based on cash on hand, plus the item cash due from banks.

Rather elaborate provisions were made for the incorporation of trust companies in the State Bank Law of 1905. These institutions were also referred to as bank and trust companies. They were permitted to perform regular banking functions as well as fiduciary functions. Extensive provisions were also made for the incorporation of savings banks.

Instead of creating a separate department of banking to manage the new system, the Texas Legislature sought to economize by adding the work of bank supervision to the duties of the Commissioner of Agriculture, Insurance, Statistics and History. A Superintendent of Banking was simply established within this existing department. The Commissioner was allowed $500 extra compensation for his work of supervising the new state banks, and the employment of four examiners at an annual salary of $2,000 each and traveling expenses were authorized.

Thus the Legislature reestablished a state banking system in response to a mandate from the people, after thirty years of prohibition of state banks. The new system was destined to live much longer than the crude banking systems created under the Constitution of 1869 or the general banking law of 1874. The principle of publicly regulated banks had become thoroughly established in America and had now set roots in Texas. To the history of this restored state banking system, we may now direct our attention.

The first state bank chartered in Texas under the State Bank Law of 1905 was the Union Bank and Trust Company of Houston, which commenced operations on August 21, 1905. This institution received charter No. 1, dated August 14, 1905. Its capital was $500,000. The first state bank to commence business, however, was the American Bank and Trust Company of Houston, which received charter No. 2 but had commenced business on August 16, 1905 with a capital of $100,000. The Bank of Somerville received charter No. 4 but also commenced business on August 16, 1905. Its capital was $10,000. The American Bank and Trust Company of San Antonio, which received charter No. 3, was reported to have commenced business on August 23, 1905, with a capital of $100,000. All of these institutions filed their charters on August 14, 1905, the day the Texas State Bank Law became effective.

The Superintendent of Banking made his first official call for a statement of condition on September 30, 1905, less than seven weeks after the state system had been restored. At that time there were twenty-two banks of discount and deposit, and seven trust companies who reported on their financial condition. The next official report on January 3, 1906, indicated thirty-five banks and eight trust companies in operation under the new law. The third report indicated sixty-five banks and fourteen trust companies on April 2, 1906. August 13, 1906 found ninety-four banks and eighteen trust companies, while on October 31, 1906, the numbers had climbed to one hundred fifteen banks and twenty-one trust companies in operation in Texas.

By the close of the year December 20, 1906, a total of 157 financial institutions had been incorporated under the new Texas State Bank Law. One of these was a savings bank, twenty-one were trust companies and one hundred thirty-five were banks of deposit and discount. Their combined capital was $5,616,500. The extremely rapid growth of state banks in Texas the early twentieth century demonstrates the demand that had developed for banks after decades of distrust and the confidence the public had developed in a state system of banks.

The new state banking system appeared to be developing two distinct institutions — the commercial type of bank and the trust company. It appeared as though the trust company was making remarkable advancement in Texas during the first year of the new system. A close examination of their official reports, however, indicates that their major business was primarily the receiving of deposits and the making of loans and discounts. Although these companies were known as "trust companies" or "bank and trust companies," their trust business was negligible in character. They were essentially commercial banks and were trust companies in name only.

H. N. Tinker, vice president of the Union Bank and Trust Company of Houston appears to have been the first banker in Texas to take a decidedly active interest in the promotion of trust banking. At the meeting of the American Bankers Association in Chicago in 1909, he reported that Texas had the following membership in the trust section of this organization:

Fig. 7

Year	Membership
1906	9
1907	18
1908	21
1909	26

At the Los Angeles meeting the following year, he reported that "Texas is making rapid strides in extending trust company facilities in almost every town of importance. There are now about seventy-five trust companies in Texas, although the law authorizing them is only five years old." As early as 1911, N. S. Graham of San Antonio reported to the American Bankers Association that "there is a gradual growth of the trust feature in Texas." However, at the 1918 meeting of the ABA, Tom F. Rogers of Denison reported that there were seventy trust companies in Texas, with total resources amounting to over $65,000,000. He contended that "the seventy trust companies carry very little business of a fiduciary character. Most of them, while having the word 'trust' as part of their corporate title, are in fact banks, and confine their operations to that of regular banking. They are simply commercial banks with the word 'trust' in their title." The state banks of Texas have never performed an extensive trust function in connection with commercial banking.

The expansion of the state banks under the Law of 1905 is set forth in Figure 8, compiled from the official reports of the Commissioner of Insurance and Banking from 1905 to date. Figure 8 reveals that a total of 1,560 state banking institutions had been organized under the Texas State Bank Law of 1905 by the close of 1928. At that time 810 institutions had closed and there had been 228 failures, leaving only 750 state banking institutions in operation. The maximum expansion of the state banking system occurred in 1921, when there were 1,025 state institutions in operation. It is clear upon examination of the figures that the restored state banking system mushroomed during the first fifteen years of its existence.

Since 1921, however, the number of state banks in operation has decreased materially. The failure rate among Texas state banks was extremely low until 1921. Beginning with that year, there were thirty-four failures. This was followed by twenty-two failures in 1922, fifteen in 1923, and twenty-two in 1924. The immediate cause of these failures was the depression in the prices of cotton and other agricultural products. The fundamental cause was likely the unsound banking policies encouraged by the existence of the depositor's guaranty system,

Fig. 8

EVOLUTION OF TEXAS STATE BANKS, 1906 – 1928

Year	Organized	Closed	Failed
1906	157	1	0
1907	375	29	3
1908	606	22	8
1911	764	91	10
1912	839	111	11
1913	963	131	11
1914	1,017	150	15
1915	1,040	211	18
1916	1,066	231	21
1917	1,109	245	22
1918	1,145	257	23
1919	1,205	287	25
1920	1,312	301	34
1921	1,359	334	68
1922	1,386	400	90
1923	1,407	457	105
1924	1,438	497	127
1925	1,460	621	178
1926	1,500	694	208
1927	1,506	741	223
1928	1,560	810	228

which provided a sort of mental insurance for depositors and encouraged reckless practices on the part of the management of numerous state banks. The maximum number of failures occurred in 1925, when fifty-one state banks went to the wall. The next year thirty institutions failed and in 1927, fifteen state banks suspended operations. This produced a critical situation in Texas and resulted in conversion to the national system by many state banks in order to escape the growing burdens of the depositor's guaranty system. Between 1919 and 1926, 120 state banks were converted to the national system, where they hoped they would enjoy the rising prestige of national banks. This critical situation gave rise to a more antagonistic examination of the guaranty system. People began to realize that this panacea for the ills of the system, this substitute for sound bank administration, had failed in the hour of its greatest need. It had proven to be an economic mirage.

The principle of insurance of bank deposits was adopted in Texas largely as the result of political agitation, inspired in part by William J. Bryan in the presidential campaign of 1908. Mr. Bryan addressed the Texas Legislature by invitation on April 5, 1909. He argued with his usual enthusiasm concerning the sanctity of platform pledges and the advantages of a bank guaranty system. Sound scholarship, however, among the nation's leading economists and financiers condemned the scheme everywhere. The Texas Legislature and the political leaders of the state characteristically ignored the advice of the country's leading financial experts. They spurned the opinions of the state's prominent bankers.

Time has demonstrated, however, even to the satisfaction of those detractors who are still alive, the folly of sacrificing scientific reasoning for political emotionalism. In common with most legislative bodies and public leaders, the statesmen of 1910 erroneously believed that they could upset fundamental economic laws by a single legislative act. The objections to the principle of state insurance of bank deposits were probably best summarized by the United States Comptroller of the Currency in 1923 in the following language:

> Insurance is sound as a protection against un-
> avoidable hazards, but dangerous whenever it
> tends to increase the hazard. The guaranty of bank
> deposits, tends to increase the hazard by eliminat-
> ing the value of character as a banker's asset. It
> tends to make all banks look alike to the public
> and to put the careful conservative banker, who is
> unwilling to make large promises and to take large
> chances, at a disadvantage. The theory is at fault
> in placing more emphasis upon the payment of
> deposits after a bank has failed, than upon prevent-
> ing failure. Its weakness always develops in a crisis.

This characterization of the bank deposit insurance scheme seems to fit the experience in Texas exactly. The weakness of the guaranty system in this state developed in the depression of 1921. The net loss in the history of the Texas guaranty system was $12,257,972.74 according to Commissioner James Shaw. The result of the increased cost on the banks for the support of the guaranty fund during the last months of its existence was a wholesale desertion of the state banking system. In the first six months of 1925, sixty-eight state banks converted to national banks. In total during 1925, seventy-six state banks followed suit. In 1921, twenty-three state banks consolidated. By 1926, fifty-three consolidations had occurred. In addition to the failures, consolidations and conversions, thirty state banks voluntarily liquidated between 1921 and 1926. The deposit guaranty system was a failure in Texas.

Numerous visionary schemes were brought forth by the Legislature to solve the unfortunate situation. On February 7, 1925, a law was enacted which permitted banks to secure their depositors by depositing with the Bank Commissioner a bond approved by the Attorney General. In administering this law, the Banking Commissioner refused to accept government or municipal bonds that were part of the bank's assets, since this proposal did not provide additional security above the general assets of the banks. To accept government bonds which were also carried on the bank's books as part of its general assets would nullify the principle of deposit insurance in the state. This procedure would give the depositors little, if any, protection over the system where no deposit insurance existed. In enacting this law, the Legislature committed another of the numerous blunders in financial legislation for which Texas Legislatures have been noted, by failing to specify the *type* of bond to be deposited with the Bank Commissioner. A surety bond is vastly different from a government or municipal bond, but the Legislature failed to indicate what kind of a bond was intended.

The Texas Bank and Trust Company of Austin accordingly carried a case to Supreme Court of Texas to determine whether the Legislature meant a surety bond, or any municipal or Government bond. The Court concluded that Article 475 of the Revised Statutes of Texas warranted "the deposit of government, municipal or state bonds with the Bank Commissioner, notwithstanding the bonds constituted a part of the assets of the bank." By permitting the deposit of government and municipal bonds, which are also part of the assets of a bank, and not bonds provided in addition to such assets, the principal of depositor's insurance vanished from the Texas law. To deposit these assets with the bank Commissioner provided no additional insurance. Deposit insurance among Texas banks was dead.

Thus by a shrewd piece of political trickery, through careful use of the English language, depositors were deprived of insurance. At the same time, the members of the Legislature could point to each other and to the Supreme Court and ask, "Who killed Cock Robin?" In January 1927, the Legislature recognized the utter failure of the deposit insurance scheme which had been set up seventeen years before by repealing the entire law. This action revealed and terminated the most outstanding weakness in the Texas state banking system.

Another weakness of the Texas state banking system was the policy of the state in failing to provide adequate supervision and inspection of these banks. Texas Legislatures have been notoriously negligent in providing funds for the supervision of banking institutions. With the tendency toward reckless banking engendered by insurance of bank deposits, supervision by the state should have been extremely careful. Had the Legislature been as generous in providing support for bank supervision prior to 1920 as they have been recently, it is probable that the history of state banks in Texas would have been far less depressing. The lesson concerning the need for adequate supervision has been learned but mastered too late to save many a depositor's hard-earned money.

A further fundamental error was made in 1923, upon the establishment of the Department of Banking, by the failure to include provisions for the publication of annual or biennial official reports for this branch of the government. As a result, the people are, to a large extent, kept in the dark regarding the operation of the state banking system. It would seem rational that in this enlightened day, the citizens of Texas should have full and complete information concerning their state banks. Startling though it may seem, it must be noted that this writer met with greater difficulty in gathering facts on the Texas state banking system since 1920, than for all the years preceding that date.

NATIONAL BANKS

The first appearance of a national bank in Texas occurred on September 22, 1865 when the First National Bank of Galveston was established with a capital of $200,000. This institution was set up by men with interests in Ball, Hutchings & Company, and McMahan & Gilbert, private bankers. George Sealy of the former became vice president of the First National Bank, while Thomas H. McMahan became president of the new institution.

That the first bank established in Texas under the National Bank Act of 1863 commanded the confidence of the people is indicated by the fact that its total deposits exceeded $385,000 on October 1, 1866. It had no overdraft and had limited its loans and discounts to less than $103,000. To protect its depositors, it carried a surplus of $4,000 and undivided profits exceeding $28,000 in addition to its $200,000 capital. The foundation for national banks was thus laid on a conservative basis in the period of social disorganization following the Civil War. To provide a sound currency following the recent unfortunate experience with Confederate inflation, wildcat banknotes and various types of shinplasters, $170,000 in national bank notes were put into circulation by this bank. Today, this institution continues to operate with a capital and surplus of $400,000. It is the oldest national bank in Texas.

The National Bank of Texas, organized at Galveston under a charter dated March 9, 1866, was the second national bank established in this state with original capital of $100,000. Ebenezer B. Nichols, a financial agent of the Confederate States, was selected as president and William T. Clark, a former major in the Union Army, became cashier. Ten of the directors were former Confederate officers. The bank established connections with the northeast through the National Park Bank of New York City. That this bank was prepared to meet any demands of its depositors for cash is indicated by its balance sheet as of October 1, 1866. Its cash reserve, including the amounts due from other banks, was nearly as large as its total deposits. A reserve to deposit ratio of ten to twenty is usually considered ample for national banks. However, this bank was operating in a notably unstable period in Texas history and its management were acutely aware of the times in which they were living and conducting business. Thus, it was prepared to meet a run should the depositors suddenly lose confidence. This bank continued in operation until March 19, 1890, when it voluntarily liquidated.

The assets the National Bank of Texas were taken over by W. L. Moody & Company, a firm of private bankers. W. L. Moody had moved to Galveston from Freestone County at the close of the Civil War and had engaged in the cotton commission business with L. F. Moody. Like all cotton commission merchants of that day, this firm found it necessary to receive deposits, make loans and carry on some banking functions for their customers in the interior of Texas. In 1870, the firm of Moody, Bradley & Company was organized to succeed W. L. Moody & L. F. Moody. This concern in turn was succeeded in 1872 by Moody & Jamison and finally by W. L. Moody & Company, private bankers. The members of this firm owned practically all the stock in the National Bank of Texas and, on the dissolution of this institution in 1890, they took over the assets. The firm of W. L. Moody & Company, Bankers, continues in Galveston to this day as a private bank.

Eight more national banks were chartered in Texas between March 1866 and 1873. The First National Bank at Houston was chartered March 22, 1866. This institution merged with the private bank of B. A. Shepherd in 1867. The San Antonio National Bank was chartered on July 30, 1866 with Mr. George W. Brackenridge as its first president. These two banks continue operation at the present time.

The first appearance of an overdraft in a Texas national bank was recorded in the report of the National Bank of Jefferson in October 1871, not long after the bank was granted its charter. Although this bank was ultra-conservatively managed, it went into the hands of a receiver on June 24, 1896.

The final three national banks organized during the period of Reconstruction in Texas were the National Exchange Bank of

Houston, the First National Bank of Denison and the First National Bank at Austin. All were established in the first seven months of 1873.

These banks earned profits that averaged considerably higher than the average for national banks in the rest of the United States. During the seven-year period of Reconstruction from October 1866 to October 1873, the aggregate resources of these national banks increased from slightly less than $1,370,000 to almost $2,870,000. The deposits increased from approximately $731,000 to $1,195,000 during the same period. This indicates that Texans were far more prosperous during the latter part of Reconstruction than historians have since generalized southern people.

The development of national banks in Texas is presented in Figure 9 using relevant data compiled from the official reports of the United States Comptroller of the Currency:

Fig. 9

EVOLUTION OF NATIONAL BANKS IN TEXAS 1874 – 1893

Year Ending November 1	Banks Organized	Banks Closed	Capital
1874	10	0	$1,115,000
1877	12	0	$1,125,000
1880	15	1	$1,420,000
1883	48	2	$3,966,000
1886	79	5	$7,615,000
1889	142	8	$15,229,000
1891	222	15	$25,762,000
1893	254	32	$25,926,000

In 1889, Texas saw more national banks organized than any other state. In that year, thirty-six new national banks organized. The following year, Texas again headed the list with sixty-three new national banks. These new institutions represented a banking capital of $5,950,000. Only ten new national banks were chartered in 1893. The unfavorable economic conditions leading up to the Panic of 1893 were probably partly responsible for the sudden checking of national bank promotion.

The high point of national bank promotion in Texas was reached in the year ending October 30, 1890, when 205 national banks had been organized and 194 were in operation. But by the following year, fifteen national banks in the state had closed their doors. People had begun to realize that even national banks were not infallible.

The first bank under the national banking system to fail in Texas was the First National Bank of Dallas, which failed on June 8, 1878, after a career of only four years. The cause of the failure, as given by the Comptroller of the Currency, was "injudicious banking and depreciation of securities." A unique result of this failure is that there has not been a First National Bank *of* Dallas since, as the Comptroller made it a rule never to permit a new banking house to use the corporate title of a defunct bank. The institution resulting from the merger of the American Exchange National and City National Banks, however, is now known as the First National Bank *in* Dallas, the difference in the moniker consisting of but one word.

From 1874 to 1893, the total resources of national banks in Texas increased from approximately $3,500,000 to $68,500,000. During this period, national banks in Texas did a voluminous business. The ratio of dividends to capital averaged 10.18 for Texas national banks, while the average for the United States was only 8.21. The ratio of earnings to capital and surplus for Texas was 12.05, while the average for the United States was but 7.86. Texas was an attractive field for national banks between the close of Reconstruction and the Panic of 1893.

The state made rapid strides forward in her economic and social life between the Panic of 1873 and the Panic of 1893. Texas people caught the spirit of social reform represented by the Granger movement that brooded over the entire nation in the 1870s and 1880s. In 1890, the greenback movement was succeeded by the populist agitation. This uprising was soon converted into the free silver advocacy which came so near to sweeping Mr. W. J. Bryan into the Presidency in 1896, and which finally spent its force in the presidential campaign of 1900. These politico-economic uprisings were all part of the same essential demand. They were a widespread cry for better economic conditions for the agricultural classes through cheap money. Texas bankers for the most part were opposed to the cheap money theories of that day. Their public utterances on various occasions reveal that they believed free silver to be a false philosophy. Time has substantially demonstrated the correctness of their views.

The grave political error made by the pioneers of 1876, when they reincorporated anti-bank language into the State Constitution, to bind posterity as well as themselves was daily becoming self-evident at the close of the nineteenth century. This policy resulted in the development of national banks as the only chartered banks in the state at this time. The national banks made greater growth in Texas as a result of the prohibition of state banks. The Fannin County Bank of Bonham, chartered by the state under the Constitution of 1869, ceased to function as a state bank in 1898. Thereafter, Texas had no state banks again until 1905. By 1900, the national banks had become so numerous that they virtually dominated banking affairs in Texas.

While there was a slight decrease in the number of national banks in operation after 1894, the dawn of the twentieth century witnessed a strong revival of national bank promotion. Since 1900, each succeeding year has experienced a gradual increase in the number of these institutions in operation. In 1900, in response to the recommendations of currency comptroller James E. Eckels, the U.S. Congress provided for the organization of national banks with a capital of $25,000 instead of $50,000, which had been the minimum capital allowed since the system was created in 1863. This permitted the organization of national banks in many small communities in Texas that had previously been unable to raise the minimum $50,000 capital. The effect of this reduction in the capital requirements

Fig. 10

EVOLUTION OF NATIONAL BANKS IN TEXAS 1894 – 1928

Year Ending November 1	Banks Organized	Banks Closed	Capital
1894	258	40	$23,230,000
1899	278	79	$19,205,000
1904	524	103	$31,284,000
1909	693	171	$42,533,000
1914	770	241	$52,239,000
1919	832	279	$58,473,000
1924	918	334	$74,542,000
1928	1047	395	$83,635,000

of national banks was immediately noticed in the rapid increase in the number of national banks in Texas. It was now possible to organize a national bank in the smaller communities of the state, where the people had only the less-stable private banks on which to depend. This change was a fortunate turn of events for Texas at this period in her banking history.

The failure rate has been very low among national banks in this state. The latter half of 1893, following the panic of that year, resulted in the closing of three national banks in Texas. While five national banks closed during 1894, only two of these were failures. Two failures of small banks out of 218 national banks in operation in 1894 was a remarkable record in sound banking. During the following year, nine national banks closed but only three of these represented failures. By the close of 1896, Texas had experienced a total of twenty-one bank failures among national banks. This is a testament to conservative bank management, when one considers that 263 national banks had been organized in the state. By 1914, a total of thirty-one national banks had failed. By 1918, there were thirty-four failures.

Since World War I, national banks have further revealed their strength by the small number of failures among them, as can

Fig. 11

Year	Failures
1919	0
1920	0
1921	5
1922	2
1923	1
1924	1
1927	10
1928	2

be seen in Figure 11. There were no failures during the period of high prices and inflation in 1919 and 1920. Those failures which did happen occurred as a result of the financial and industrial depression experienced at the close of the World War. When the large number of national banks in existence is considered and the extensive economic diversification in Texas is taken into account, it becomes readily apparent that the national banks of Texas exhibited a notable record of safety.

The number of national banks in operation during the thirteen years prior to the close of the World War modestly increased from 488 to 543. Why was the growth of national banks stunted during this period relative to their rapid growth during the 1890s? With Texas expanding along many industrial lines and economic life becoming increasingly diversified and complex, this is a reasonable inquiry. The answer is found in the restoration of the state banking system and the burst of growth of state banks after 1905. Under the Texas State Bank Law of 1905, it was much easier to raise the required capital to establish a state bank than it was to raise capital for a national bank.

The state system was also popular because of the false peace of mind provided by the depositor's guaranty system set up on May 12, 1909, at the urgent behest of William J. Bryan. Greater profits, increased efficiency and less exacting supervision were promised to bankers who incorporated under the state system.

While Texas depositors had no reason to complain of the safety of the national banks, the wild promises of safety included in the scheme of deposit insurance, appealed to the imagination of many persons. As a result, whenever a new bank was chartered in Texas it was usually a state bank. The people, however, were doomed to bitter disappointment in the safety of depositor's insurance.

Another test of the success of a bank is its dividend rate. Information on this subject is not available for the state banks. In fact, very little information of a statistical character is available concerning state banks, especially in the last few years. For the national banks, however, the Comptroller of the Currency published elaborate figures on earnings of these institutions. From 1894 to 1905, the average dividend on capital for the national banks in Texas was 9.09 percent, while the figure for the United States was 7.93 percent. On the basis of capital and surplus for the same period, Texas national banks averaged 7.80 percent, while the national banks of the nation averaged only 5.5 percent. The ratio of net earnings to capital during this period averaged 11.10 percent for Texas and 7.55 for the nation. The conclusion is inescapable that national banks in Texas from 1894 until the restoration of the state banking system were highly prosperous institutions.

From 1906 to 1918, the rural national banks in Texas earned considerably more profit than the average earnings of national banks in the United States. According to the classification of the Comptroller of the Currency, all banks in Texas outside of the cities of Dallas, Fort Worth, Galveston, Houston, San Antonio and Waco were known as country banks. The average ratio of dividends to capital in the country banks for the thirteen years was 12.69 percent, while the average for the United States was only 11.57 percent. Similarly, the ratio of dividends to capital and surplus in Texas was 8.4.9 percent as compared with 6.98 percent for the United States. On the basis of net earnings to capital and surplus, the Texas banks averaged 12.12 percent, while the average for the United States was 9.71 percent.

For the period 1919 to 1928 inclusive, the figures on earnings of country national banks in Texas reveal a rather startling situation. During this ten year period, the ratio of dividends to capital was 10.82 percent for Texas, and 12.84 for the United States. On the basis of dividends to capital and surplus the Texas ratio averaged 6.84 percent while that for the United States was the same. That the national banks have been prosperous as a class is clearly apparent. During the past ten years, however, the country national banks in Texas for the first time in their long career averaged a lower dividend.

FEDERAL INSTITUTIONS

The Federal Reserve System, established by the United States Congress on December 23, 1913, provided the unifying influence for banking in Texas. This state was included in the Eleventh Federal Reserve district, and the Federal Reserve Bank was opened at Dallas November 16, 1914, in temporary quarters on the main floor of an old bank building at 1305 Main Street. The Eleventh Federal Reserve District included all of the state of Texas, a small portion of southern Oklahoma, western Louisiana, eastern New Mexico and a small strip of territory in Arizona. This banking district is a great empire in itself. It constitutes a territory greater in area than the regions served by the Bank of England, the Bank of France, or the Reichsbank of Berlin. The Federal Reserve Bank at Dallas is very similar to these central banks in Europe, after which it was patterned. It is essentially a banker's bank, or a bank for banks.

Without the blare of trumpets, a street parade or an orgy of advertising, the modest-appearing Federal Reserve Bank at Dallas inaugurated a new epoch in the financial history of the southwest. One Dallas newspaper published in its Sunday edition a picture of the board of directors and officers, together with a short account of the forthcoming opening the next day. More publicity was given to the breaking of ground for a new boulevard in Dallas than to the inauguration of the most far-reaching financial reformation in the history of the southwest.

Promptly at 10 a.m. on the appointed day, the doors of the great institution swung open and it sprung to life. For several weeks prior to the formal opening, the clerical force and executives had been engaged in organizing the institution and preparing for active operation. Oscar Wells of Houston became the first governor of this bank. In March 1915, he was succeeded by R. L. Van Zandt of Fort Worth, a son of the venerable banker, Major K. M. Van Zandt and a grandson of Isaac Van Zandt of the Republic of Texas. The institution was organized by and is still controlled by native Texans.

Open house was observed the first day. The general public was invited to visit the bank and meet the officers, and in the evening a banquet was held for the visiting bankers in the city. Thus, almost without formal ceremony, the institution that was destined to revolutionize the financial activities of the southwest modestly began its service to the economic development of this great territory.

On the second day of business, the bank received $2,000,000 in Federal Reserve Bank Notes from the Secretary of the Treasury for use in the rediscounting of commercial paper. Large shipments of gold were received by express during the first two days from member banks in the district. The institution had previously announced that they would accept gold or silver from member banks to meet the required reserve deposits. However, since the Reserve did not have the physical facilities for the storage of large quantities of silver, it would pay the express charges only when the member banks shipped gold.

At the first meeting of the board of directors on the opening day, the rediscount rates were reduced from 6 and 6.5 percent, to 5.5 and 6 percent, on 30-day and 90-day paper respectively. The board of directors felt that this lower rate was more appropriate for Texas and they assumed the Federal Reserve Board at Washington would sustain the action. Thus, on that very first day, the question of the authority of the Federal Reserve Board to control the rediscount rate in each of the twelve districts was raised by the Dallas institution.

While all the national banks in the district were required to join the system, the state banks of Texas were slow in availing themselves of the services of the Federal Reserve Bank at Dallas. The Texas Legislature, on September 11, 1914, appealed to the Federal Reserve Board at Washington to hasten the establishment of the regional reserve banks in order to save the cotton farmers from disasters incident to falling prices. The Legislature assured the Board that the Texas state banks would actively cooperate with the system to meet the financial crisis in the cotton market. However, only ten state banks in Texas joined the system prior to 1917 despite the fact that on

October 19, 1914, the state had enacted a law authorizing the state banks to affiliate with the Federal Reserve system. About 17 percent of Texas state banks were ineligible to join the Federal Reserve system, though, because of the $25,000 minimum capital stock requirement. Furthermore, many of the state bankers felt that they could secure little benefit from the Federal Reserve system, since much of their paper was ineligible for rediscount. Many of the notes in their note cases were too small for profitable rediscount, while other loans were for capital purposes and not self-liquidating in character. Since the Texas state banks loaned on cattle and cotton, much of their paper extended over ninety days. Many state bankers were not entirely convinced of the merits of the system and simply preferred to remain free of its influence. In 1918, state law was further amended to enable the state banking system to function more harmoniously with the Federal Reserve system.

The work of the Federal Reserve Bank at Dallas developed rapidly. Applications for branches were received from enterprising cities of the district. The Federal Reserve Board has wisely discouraged the policy of opening new branches simply to gratify civic pride. It has always insisted that genuine banking needs should be the deciding factor in the establishment of branches. On June 17, 1918, a branch was opened at El Paso to serve the Arizona and New Mexico portion of the district, as well as the western portion of Texas. Because of its great distance from Dallas, the establishment of a branch at El Paso appeared justified. Sixty member banks were immediately transferred from the head office at Dallas to the El Paso branch. The third floor of the First National Bank building was used as temporary quarters. Its permanent home was occupied beginning August 15, 1920.

On August 4, 1919, another branch was opened at Houston to serve the large territory in the southern part of the state. The Dallas bank transferred 101 member banks to this district. This branch, under the management of Sam R. Lander who had opened the El Paso branch, soon outgrew its temporary quarters in the Hermann building and on February 14, 1922, moved to its new permanent home. The third branch was established at San Antonio on July 5, 1927, which included fifty-five counties in the southwest part of the state. A site for its permanent home was secured in 1927.

Thus the Federal Reserve system was completely established in Texas by 1928. Its value to Texas will have to be left to the impartial judgment of history. Today, the Federal Reserve system in Texas may well be characterized as the Commercial and Agricultural Bank at Galveston was referred to in the 1850s, as "an engine of great power" which noiselessly pumps the lifeblood of credit through the state and the national banks, into the channels of commerce of the great southwest.

Banking facilities have been provided for Texas agriculture concerns, as well. In 1916, Congress attempted to provide financial facilities for the agricultural classes of the country by creating the Federal Farm Land Banks under the Federal Farm Loan Act. The act also provided for the organization of national farm loan associations and for joint stock land banks.

When the Federal Farm Loan Board was organized, the state of Texas was constituted District No. 10 and the Federal Land Bank was located at Houston. Texas is the only state with a land bank entirely to itself. All other banks of this character serve two or more states. Apparently, the Federal Farm Loan Board was convinced that the diversification of economic interests was sufficiently great in Texas to warrant the location of a bank for this state alone.

Accordingly, the bank was established at Houston on March 26, 1917 with a capital of $750,000, approximately 95 percent of which was originally subscribed by the government. The remaining 5 percent was subscribed by local interests. The government stock was gradually retired, leaving the bank in the hands of private owners after 1924. This institution has enjoyed a steady growth since its organization. By the close of 1928, it had loaned nearly $182,000,000 at low rates of interest to more than 62,000 farmers. Fortunately, Texas escaped the land speculation that prevailed in 1919 in Iowa and a few adjoining agricultural states. Consequently, the Houston bank was not embarrassed by the falling prices that characteristically follow a land boom. The president of the institution estimates that the bank is saving the farmers more than $5,000,000 in annual interest rates alone, while supplying the capital needs of the farmers and ranchmen of Texas.

A number of joint stock land banks have been organized in Texas under the Federal Farm Loan Act of 1916. In January 1924, there were five joint stock banks operating in Texas. They were as follows:

(1) First Texas Joint Stock Land Bank, Houston, chartered April 23, 1919.

(2) Dallas Joint Stock Land Bank, Dallas, chartered July 3, 1919.

(3) First Trust Joint Stock Land Bank, Dallas, chartered July 5, 1922.

(4) San Antonio Joint Stock Land Bank, San Antonio, chartered September 15, 1919.

(5) Texas-Oklahoma Joint Stock Land Bank, San Antonio, chartered March 26, 1923.

During 1925 the last named bank was taken over by the Dallas Joint Stock Land Bank and the Wichita Federal Land Bank. This bank was unfortunately located, as the region around San Antonio was hardly sufficient to support two institutions of this kind. Similarly, the establishment of two joint stock land banks in Dallas proved undesirable and on November 30, 1928, the First Trust Joint Stock Land Bank at Dallas was merged with a similar bank in Chicago. At the present time, there are three of these institutions operating in Texas, one in Houston, one in Dallas, and one in San Antonio. These institutions loan their funds primarily on real estate.

In order to meet the obvious needs among the agricultural classes for short-term credit, Congress enacted the Agricultural Credit Act of 1923, creating the National Agricultural Credit

Corporation and providing for the organization of twelve Federal Intermediate Credit Banks. These institutions were to operate in close affiliation with the Federal Land Banks. The activities of these banks are confined to discounting paper for private loan companies, cooperative marketing associations, cooperative banks and other banks which serve the farmers.

The Intermediate Credit Bank for Texas was established at Houston. In 1928, there were eighteen loan companies which had qualified to rediscount their paper with this bank. Since the bank does not deal directly with farmers and ranchers, some ranchers believe that the institutions were created primarily to serve just the cattle companies rather than the cattle industry as a whole. Farmers and ranchers are able to avoid the private companies to a limited extent by working through cooperative marketing associations. A fine example of such an association, the Texas Farm Bureau Cotton Association, has made remarkable growth recently. The Texas Cotton Growers Finance Corporation, started in 1924 as a subsidiary of the former.

While the Federal Government and numerous bankers have made special efforts to help the farmer by liberal extension of credit, farmers as a group are still in a precarious situation. The Texas cotton grower is now in greater need of capital and credit than he is in need of banking facilities. Except for loans on land, the farmer, is still subject to high and extortionate interest rates.

CONCLUSION

Texas bankers have been prominent in American banking for three score years and ten. Throughout the history of banking in America, Texas bankers have played a leading role. Beginning with the opening of the Commercial and Agricultural Bank at Galveston in 1847 by Samuel May Williams, the bankers of this state have been faithful public servants. In the face of misguided and exasperating political controversies involving monetary and banking problems, Texas bankers have built quietly and steadily on the rock of public confidence. They have erected a banking structure that is a credit to our people. From the days of McMahan and Rosenberg of Galveston, Shepherd of Houston and Brackenridge of San Antonio to the venerable C. B. Dorchester of Sherman and K. M. Van Zandt of Fort Worth, men whose lives have been coextensive with the history of Texas banking, the financial fraternity in this state has rendered a public service that has been indispensable to the social life of the people.

From an historical study of the activities of Texas bankers, we find that they have always been loyal to the best interests of the state. At the annual meetings of the American Bankers Association, since its organization in 1875, Texas bankers have always been in attendance and have been a credit to Texas. They have no doubt been influential in placing the state before the world in a truthful light. Service to the whole state has been the goal of these men, who have always sought to develop the economic interests of the entire commonwealth. Agriculture, manufacturing and numerous other economic interests necessary to develop a diversified economic life have always received the wholehearted support of the splendid public servants known as the bankers of Texas.

The monetary and banking history of this state is rich in economic and financial lore. Texas has passed through nearly all the stages of economic life in the last century. The growth of her monetary institutions has retraced the evolution of monetary and banking theories the world over. The history of her banking institutions represents an excellent cross-section of American banking history. The lessons in finance taught by our history, from the Mexican regime to the present day, are principles of worldwide value.

Today, in some sections of the state, the old and the new forms of social life flourish together. The private bank, the state bank, the loan shark, the pawnbroker, the investment institution and the national bank flourish side-by-side, often in the same block. In social and economic life, the rustic nature of pioneer days and the progressiveness of the modern world are found together in the same cities. A state of economic contrasts, Texas throughout her long history has contributed valuable lessons to monetary and banking science.

Let it be hoped that the great teachings in public and private finance given to the world by the banking history of Texas will be preserved for posterity. Through historical evolution, social life in Texas today has reached a high plane of intelligence and responsibility, a status that reflects honor on the pioneers who founded the Republic, credit on the men who built the state, and glory on all people who love the name of Texas.

A TEXAS BANKING HISTORY TIMELINE

1835 – Samuel May Williams obtains charter from the Mexican authorities for the *Banco de Commercia y Agricultura*.

1836 – Republic of Texas officially recognizes the charter for the Commercial & Agricultural Bank.

1839 – Congress of the Republic of Texas rejects a bill that would establish a national bank for the Republic.

1841 – Congress of the Republic of Texas authorizes the firm of McKinney & Williams to issue $30,000 in notes to circulate as currency.

1844 – Congress of the Republic of Texas repeals the law authorizing the issue of paper money by McKinney & Williams, or any other entity.

1845 – First State Constitution prohibits the formation of banks and the issue of paper money.

1847 – The Commercial & Agricultural Bank opens at Galveston.

1854 – B. A. Shepherd of Houston and Ball, Hutchings & Company of Galveston begin acting as commission, exchange & collection agents in their respective locations.

1859 – Commercial & Agricultural Bank closes after years of legal battles challenging its activities and charter.

1863 – National Bank Act is enacted in the United States.

1865 – The first bank to be chartered in Texas under the National Bank Act, the First National Bank of Galveston, is chartered.

1869 – The state Constitution allows for the state charter of banks for the first time. Charters were to be granted by special acts of the Legislature.

1874 – The general banking law of 1874 allows for the general incorporation of state banks through the Secretary of State.

1876 – State-chartered banks are again constitutionally prohibited.

1905 – The State Bank Law enacted this year made state banks legal and created a regulated state bank system.

1914 – Federal Reserve Bank of Dallas opens.

1916 – Federal Farm Loan Act creates Federal Farm Land Banks.

1917 – Federal Land Bank of Houston is organized.

1925 – The formation of new private banks is prohibited by an act of the State Legislature and existing private banks became subject to state regulation.

GENERAL BIBLIOGRAPHY

1. Adams, Ephraim Douglas. *British Diplomatic Correspondence Concerning the Republic of Texas 1838-1846.* Austin: The Texas State Historical Association, 1917.

2. American Bankers Association. *Proceedings.* New York: 1882-1916.

3. Austin, C. O. *Texas Banker's Record,* January (1926): 2.

4. Austin Papers. Texas State Library.

5. Babcock, Frederick N. *The Appraisal of Real Estate.* Chicago: Macmillan Company, 1924.

6. Bancroft, H. H. *History of the North American States and Texas.* The History Company. San Francisco, 1889.

7. Barker, Eugene C. "The Finances of the Texas Revolution." *Political Science Quarterly,* Vol. 19 (1904): 612.

8. Johnson, Francis W. *A History of Texas and Texans.* The American Historical Society. Chicago, 1914.

9. *Banker's Magazine and Statistical Register.* New York: I. Smith Homan, Jr. Vol. 20 (1865-66)–Vol. 90 (1915).

10. Barnett, George E. "State Banking in the United States." *Historical and Political Science Studies,* Vol. 20 (1902)

11. Barnett, George E. "State Banks and Trust Companies since the passage of the National Bank Act." National Monetary Commission, 61st Congress 3rd Session. Senate Document No. 659. Washington, D. C. (1911).

12. Beckman, Theodore E. *Credit and Collections in Theory and Practice.* New York: McGraw-Hill, 1924.

13. Cable, J. R. *The Bank of the State of Missouri.* New York: Longman's Green & Company, 1923.

14. Caldwell, Mosser & Williams. *Joint Stock Land Banks with Special Reference of the San Antonio Joint Stock Land Bank.* Chicago: Privately published, 1923.

15. Carlson, Avery L. "Oklahoma Bank Failures and Agricultural Prices." *The Southwestern Political and Social Science Quarterly* Vol. V, no. 1 (1924): 72.

16. Castaneda, Carlos E. *The Mexican Side of the Texas Revolution*. Dallas: P. L. Turner Company, 1928.

17. City Directory of Saint Louis, Missouri. 1816, 1818, 1819.

18. Clark, M. H. "The Last Days of the Confederate Treasury and What Became of Its Specie." Southern Historical Society, Papers, IX (1881).

19. Coke, Governor. Message to the Texas Legislature. February 10, 1874.

20. Commissioner of Insurance. Texas. Official Reports. 1920, 1922.

21. *Campaign Textbook of the Democratic Party in Texas*. (1908): 224.

22. "Constitution of the Provisional Government of the Confederate States of America, May 21, 1861." Gammel's *Laws of Texas*. Vol. 5.

23. Texas Constitution. 1861, 1866, 1869. Gammel's *Laws of Texas*. Vol. 5, 7.

24. Congressional Record. 63rd Congress, 2nd Session. Appendix, p. 1196.

25. Cook, I. J. "Insurance of Bank Deposits in the West." *Quarterly Journal of Economics*, 24 (1909):85-108.

26. Wheaton, Henry. *Elements of International Law*. Oxford: Clarendon Press, 1866.

27. Davis, Jefferson. *The Rise and Fall of the Confederate Government*. New York: D. Appleton & Company, 1881.

28. Dewey, David Rich. *Financial History of the United States*. New York: Longman's Green & Company, 1915.

29. Edwards, David B. *The History of Texas, or Emigrant's, Farmer's and Politician's Guide*. Cincinnati: J. A. James & Co., 1836.

30. Federal Farm Loan Board. *Annual Report*. 1917–1928.

31. Fleming, Walter L. *Documentary History of Reconstruction*. Cleveland: Arthur H. Clarke Company, 1906.

32. Ford, A. W. "Country Banking Practice in Northern Texas." *Journal of Business*. April, July and October (1928)

33. *The Story of Fort Worth National Bank*. For Worth: Privately printed for the Bank, 1923.

34. First National Bank of Port Arthur. Pamphlet announcement of the new plan for industrial loans.

35. Garrison, George P. *Texas: A Contest of Civilizations*. Boston: Houghton-Mifflin, 1903.

36. General and Special Laws of Texas. 40th Legislature, 1st Called Session. 1927. Sections 2, 3, 4, 5.

37. Gossett, M. H. President Federal Land Bank, Houston. Address at Brownwood, Texas, Nov. 15, 1928, in the *Houston Post-Dispatch*, December 2, 1928.

38. Gossett, M. H. "Accomplishments of the Federal Intermediate Credit Banks." An Address before the Southwestern Political and Social Science Association, 10th Annual Convention. Austin, March 29-30, 1929.

39. Gouge, William M. *The Fiscal History of Texas*. Philadelphia: Lippincott, Grambo & Company, 1852.

40. The Southern Historical Association. *The South in the Building of the Nation*. Richmond: Southern Publication Society, 1909.

41. Harr, Luther. *Branch Banking in England*. Philadelphia: University of Pennsylvania Press, 1928.

42. Hart, Albert B. *Essentials in American History*. Chicago: American Book Company, 1905.

43. Hepburn, A. Barton. *A History of Currency in the United States*. New York: Macmillan Company, New York, 1924.

44. Herzog, Peter W. *The Morris Plan of Industrial Banking*. Chicago: A. W. Shaw Company, 1928.

45. Hibbard, Benjamin H. *Effect of the Great War Upon Agriculture in the United States and Great Britain*. New York: Oxford University Press, 1919.

46. Palgrave, H.H. *Dictionary of Political Economy*. London: Macmillan & Company, 1926.

47. Holbrook, Francis N. *Production of Gold and Silver in the United States*. Washington: Government Printing Office, 1887.

48. Hosmer, James K. *The American Civil War*. New York: Harper & Bros. New York, 1913.

49. House Journal. 30th Legislature, Texas. (1907):56.

50. Hunt, R. L. "The Problem of Short Term and Intermediate Credit." Address before the Southwestern Political and Social Science Association, Austin. March 29-30, 1929.

51. Insurance Laws of Texas. Title 24. Building and Loan Associations. Art. 867.

52. Johnston, John. "Scottish Banking System." Proceedings, 28th Annual Convention, American Bankers Association. New Orleans, 1902.

53. Journal of the Permanent Council. Republic of Texas. Published in Texas Historical Association Quarterly. Vol. 7 & 17.

54. Kennedy, William, *Texas: The Rise, Progress and Prospects of the Republic of Texas.* London: R. Hastings, 1841.

55. Kettell, Thomas P. *History of the Great Rebellion.* Worcester: L. Stebbins, 1865.

56. Kinley, David. *The Independent Treasury System of the United States.* Boston: Thomas Y. Crowell & Company, 1893.

57. Kinley, David. "Objection to Bank Deposit. Insurance." *Review of Reviews*, 37:345-7, 39:491-500.

58. Knox, John Jay. *A History of Banking in the United States.* New York: Bradford Rhodes and Company, 1900.

59. Lamar Papers. Austin: Texas State Library.

60. Laughlin, J. L. "Fallacy of Guarantee of Bank Deposits, in Latter Day Problems." *Scribner's Magazine.* 44: 101-9.

61. Laughlin, J. L. *Banking Progress.* New York: Chas. C. Scribner's Sons, 1920.

62. Lawrence, A. B. *Texas in 1840, or Emigrant's Guide to the New Republic.* New York: William A. Allen, New York, 1840.

63. Lee, V. P. "The Operation of the Texas Cotton Growers' Finance Corporation, 1926-1927." Address before the 10th Annual Meeting of the Southwestern Social and Political Science Associations. Austin, March 29-30, 1929.

64. Lee, V. P. "Farm Mortgage Financing in Texas." *Texas Agricultural Experiment Station Bulletin, No. 330, 1925.*

65. Lewis Publishing Company. *The History of Texas, together with a Biographical History of the Cities of Houston and Galveston.* Chicago: Lewis Publishing Company, Chicago, 1895.

66. Martin, Roscoe C. "The Grange as a Political Factor in Texas." *The Southwestern Political and Social Science Quarterly.* Vol. 6 (1926): 367, Vol. 30 (1927):165.

67. McAdoo, W. G. *Fort Worth Record.* November 16, 1914, p. 1.

68. Miller, Sidney L. *Railway Transportation: Principles and Point of View.* Chicago: A. W. Shaw Company, 1925.

69. Miller, Edmund Thornton. "A Financial History of Texas." *Bulletin of The University of Texas.* No. 37 (1916)

70. Morphis, J. M. *History of Texas.* New York: United States Publishing Company, 1875.

71. Moulton, Harold G. "The Surplus in Commercial Banking." *Journal of Political Economy.* Vol. 25 (1917).

72. Lincoln, Edward E. *Applied Business Finance.* Chicago: A. W. Shaw Company, 1927.

73. Muzzey, David S. *The American Adventure.* New York: Harpers & Brothers, 1927.

74. National Monetary Commission, Vol. 2, on State Banks and Trust Companies.

75. Phillips, Chester. *A Bank Credit.* New York: Macmillan Company, 1924.

76. Preston, H. H. *History of Banking in Iowa.* Iowa City: State Historical Society of Iowa, 1922.

77. Railroad Commission of Texas. 35th Annual Report. (1926)

78. Ramsdell, Charles William. "Reconstruction in Texas." *Columbia University Studies in History, Economics and Public Law.* Vol. 36. (1910)

79. Report of Special Committee on Retrenchment, February 18, 1879. Texas House Journal, 16th Legislature. First Session.

80. "Resources of the Confederacy." *Atlantic Monthly,* Vol. 88 (1901):827-838.

81. Revised Civil Statutes of Texas, (1925.) Art 475; 6146, 6167. Title 107, Art 6162, 6163, 6164, 6165.

82. Rivers, George L. *The United States and Mexico.* New York: Charles Scribner's Sons, 1913

83. *Rosenberg, Henry, 1824-1893.* Galveston: Rosenberg Library. Galveston, 1918.

84. Schouler, James. *History of the United States of America*. New York: Dodd, Mead & Co., 1894.

85. Scott, James Brown. *Cases on International Law*. St. Paul: West Publishing Company, 1922.

86. Schwulst, Earl Bryan. *Extension of Bank Credit; A Study of the Principles of Financial Statement Analysis as Applied in Extending Bank Credit to Agriculture, Industry and Trade in Texas*. Boston: Houghton-Mifflin Company, 1927.

87. Schwab, John Christopher. *The Confederate States of America, 1861-1865: A Financial and Industrial History of the South During the War*. New York: Charles Scribner's Sons, 1901.

88. Schwab, John Christopher. The Finances of the Confederate States. Yale Review, 1:175. August (1895.) Yale Review, 11:228. November. (1893.)

89. Schwab, John Christopher. Prices in the Confederate States. Political Science Quarterly. XIV. 281. June, (1899.)

90. Secretary of State, Texas. Biennial Reports; 1879, 1881, 1882, 1884, 1886, 1890, 1892. State Printers Office, Austin.

91. Shaw, James. Address before the Texas State Banker's Association. May 11, 1928. Published in The Dallas News. May 13, 1925. p. 2.

92. Snow, Freeman. *Cases and Opinions on Industrial Law*. (1893.)

93. Statistical Abstract of the United States. 1921 p. 704; 1922 p. 553; 1923 p. 645; 1924 p. 761 ; 1925 p. 274; 1926 p. 267; 1928 p. 270.

94. *Terry's Guide to Mexico*. Boston: Houghton-Mifflin Company, 1923.

95. *Texas Almanac and Emigrants Guide to Texas*. Galveston: W. Richardson & Co., 1857-1873.

96. *Texas Almanac and State Industrial Guide*. Dallas: A. H. Belo & Company. Dallas, 1910-1929.

97. Texas Bankers Association. Membership List. 1928.

98. Texas Bankers Association. *Texas Bankers Record*. September 1911 to 1929.

99. *Texas Bank & Trust Company v. Austin*. Commissioner of Banking. 280 Southwestern Reporter 161.

100. Texas Supreme Court Reports. Vol. 1., 1046 and following.

101. United States Comptroller of the Currency, Official Reports, June 30, 1863 to December 13, 1928. Published in Executive Documents of the House of Representatives 1863-4 to date.

102. *United States Department of Agriculture Year-Book.* Circular No. 88, 1915.

103. United States Census. Seventh. 1850: Eighth 1860. Mortality and Miscellaneous Statistics; Twelfth. 1900. Vol. 8; Thirteenth. 1910. Agriculture. Fourteenth. 1920. Vol. III. V. and IX.

104. Weaver, Findley. "Recent Changes in the Texas State Banking System." *Southwestern Political and Social Science Quarterly.* Vol. 8. no. 1. (1927):5.

103. Wells, Oscar. Article published in *The Fort Worth Record.* November 16, 1914. p. 1.

104. Werner, M. R. Bryan. "An American Phenomenon." Published Serially in *Liberty.* Vol. 6 No. 2. (1929).

105. *Who's Who in America. 1914-1915.* Chicago: A. W. Marquis & Co., 1915.

106. Wilson, Woodrow. *History of the American People,* New York: Harpers & Brothers, 1918.

107. Williams, Samuel May. Manuscript Collection 1819-1858. Galveston: Rosenberg Library.

108. Wooten, Dudley. *Comprehensive History of Texas: 1685 to 1895.* Dallas: William G. Scarff. Dallas, 1898.

109. Wortham, Louis J. *A History of Texas.* Forth Worth: Wortham-Molyneaux Co., 1924.

110. Yoakum, Henderson. *History of Texas.* New York: Redfield, 1856.

111. Young J. H. *New Map of Texas.* Philadelphia: L. Augustus Mitchell, Philadelphia, 1835.

NEWSPAPERS

112. Civilian & Gazette. Vol. XXI. Galveston. (1858.)

113. Dallas *Morning News*, The Vol. XIX. 1904; March 1909; April 1909; November 14-16, 1914. Published by A. H. Belo & Company, Dallas.

114. Fort Worth *Record*. Fort Worth, November 1914.

115. Galveston *Weekly News*. Vol. XIV. (1857.) Vol. XV (1858) Galveston.

116. San Antonio *Daily Herald*. San Antonio. Vol. II. (1858)

117. *Southern Intelligencer*. Vol. 3. (1858.) Austin.

118. *Star-Telegram*. July 23-30, 1922. Fort Worth.

PERSONAL LETTERS AND INTERVIEWS

119. Dorchester C. B. President Merchants and Planters National Bank, Sherman. Letter January 21, 1929.

120. Logan, Rex. Secretary-treasurer San Antonio Morris Plan Bank. Letter March 27, 1929.

121. Luton, F. L. Manager, The Morris Plan Bank of Fort Worth. Letter March 25, 1929. Interview.

122. Mehl, B. Max. Numismatists. Fort Worth. Letter March 6, 1929. Interview. April 16, 1929.

123. McCallum, Mrs. Jane Y. Secretary of State, Texas. Letter March 26, 1929.

124. Philpott, Jr. W. A. Secretary, The Texas Bankers Association. Dallas. Letter April 2, 1929.

125. Pitman, R. W. Secretary-treasurer Morris Plan Banker's Association. Saint Louis, Missouri. Letter April 1, 1929.

126. Reed, J. M. Secretary San Antonio Joint Stock Land Bank, San Antonio. Letter March 29, 1929.

127. Reichle, A. C. Cashier First National Bank, Port Arthur. Letter March 26, 1929.

128. Wright, Wilbur F. Executive Vice President Dallas Morris Plan Bank. Letter March 25, 1929.

129. Van Zandt, Khleber Miller. An Interview in his office at the Fort Worth National Bank, Fort Worth. September 19, 1928.

www.ingramcontent.com/pod-product-compliance
Lightning Source LLC
Chambersburg PA
CBHW020455100426
42813CB00031B/3376/J